FEARLESS

INSPIRING GREATNESS
FROM WITHIN

BRENLEY SHAPIRO

Editor: Randi Chapnik Myers
Cover Design: Noam Hazan

Produced by
TLAC Toronto Printing & Publishing
525 University Avenue, R5
Toronto, Ontario, M5G 2L3
www.TLAC.ca

ISBN: 978-1-7752827-0-9

Printed and bound in Canada

CONTENTS

PREFACE

Do you have hopes, goals and dreams that lie within you? Are you reaching your maximum level of attainable success? Would you like to know how to push yourself beyond the status quo and become the very best you that you can be?

Wouldn't we all? So let's learn how!

These days, it seems we are bombarded with advice on how to achieve instant success, but in reality, creating success is hard work. It's not easy to face your fears, confront challenges and connect with your passion, day in and day out. Developing your own personal sense of greatness takes time and preparation. But you can do it! When you identify and then break through the barriers that block the path toward your goals, you will be amazed at the opportunities that lie ahead.

I love the work that I do. As a Cognitive Behavioural Psychotherapist specializing in Sport and Performance, it is not only my job but also my passion to help people and teams reach their peak level of performance. Now, I am excited to share the insights, techniques and strategies I use with competitive and professional athletes, as well as other high-level performers, to help you master your mind and behaviours, and learn to adopt their same mindset. In fact, it is the process of inspiring and achieving greatness, both in myself and in others, that drove me to write this book.

My hope is that you don't just read the words in this book, but that you truly embrace the concepts and ideas within it. As you read along, you will absorb a lot of new information, so get yourself ready. Keep a journal handy to write in as you work through the exercises and answer the thought-provoking questions. You will also learn from the personal and professional stories shared about others and myself on the road to success. In doing so, you will be better equipped to foster your own personal sense of greatness and find your way to becoming fearless.

This book would never have come to life without the undying support of my family. I am grateful to my boys, Brendan and Noah, who have embraced my philosophy while putting up with my crazy schedule, and to Ryan, who picked up the slack on anything and everything at home to allow me the time to write. They have supported me in every way possible so that I could pursue my goals.

I would also like to express my gratitude to my closest friends and family who are always in my corner cheering me on and who always have my back.

Finally, a special thank you to Randi Chapnik Myers for helping me pull it all together.

CHAPTER 1
THE MILLION DOLLAR QUESTION

THE TRUTH ABOUT SUCCESS

Have you ever really stopped to think about what makes someone successful? Why do some people achieve great success while others do not? Circumstance, intelligence, talent and luck are some of the most common answers to that question. For me, it comes down to one thing: mindset.

Mindset is everything. It is the foundation upon which all is built and is ultimately what drives us. Learning to think right and shift your perspective, using the insights and strategies described in this book, will not only help you break through the barriers that are impeding your progress and holding you back, but will also teach you how to create an environment of growth and opportunity. It doesn't matter if you are in the sports world, the corporate world, a teaching or coaching environment, or just life in general; you have the power to create your greatest self and to inspire the same in those around you. Life can be an exciting journey and well worth the ride. So, get ready to become the very best you that you can be.

One day a couple of years back, my friend Stan called, asking for help. He wanted to do some mental game coaching.

"I want to run a 100-mile marathon," he told me.

Did I hear him correctly? "You want to do what?" I asked. But what I was really thinking was, *Why on earth would you want to do something like that? Are you out of your mind?* Stan has always been a very active guy, living a fit and healthy lifestyle, but he was 47 years old at the time and, unlike my regular clientele, he was not involved in any competitive sports.

Stan explained that for this particular race, runners would have 32 hours to reach the finish line—if in fact they were able to get there. Right away, my mind was buzzing with concerns. A race this long meant no rest and no sleep. People don't even engage in enjoyable activities for 32 straight hours without a break! Was he nuts? Being trained as a psychotherapist, however, I reverted back to what I do best and that was to ask a lot of questions. So that's where I began.

I started by gathering information on this type of race and on the status of Stan's current conditioning, stamina and training. I asked about the farthest distance he had ever run before. He told me that one month earlier, he had tried a 60-mile race in preparation for this one. My next question was a logical follow-up: "So, how did the 60-mile race go? How did you do?"

His answer was a little troubling. He told me that the experience was extraordinarily difficult, that he had struggled tremendously and barely finished it. But he was determined, and somehow managed to cross the finish line. "I know my ability to be successful at running the 100-mile race will be all mental," he said. "So Brenley, can you help me?"

Well? Could I? My own thoughts started running wild. *How am I supposed to help him finish a 100-mile race when he could barely finish 60? Could mental preparation and training make that much of a difference? I know that preparing athletes for competition is what I do for a living, but in this extreme situation, what if I can't make it happen?*

In this one short phone call, Stan had challenged me to my very core. I had always believed in what I do and in the difference that I can make in the lives of others by strengthening their mental game. I often stand up and speak to audiences about the power of the mind, and I even have the slogan "See It, Believe It, Achieve It" printed across the backs of the T-shirts that my staff and coaches wear. Yet, for the first time, I started to question everything I believed in. Here I was, doubting myself and all that I stood for, and I was rattled.

In the end, I decided that the only thing for me to do was to embody the skills that I teach the athletes and people I work with. It was time to make a conscious and purposeful effort to put those powerful, life-changing techniques into practice myself. Of course, until now, I thought I had always done just that. But for some reason, this time felt different.

That's when I took a deep breath and said **STOP** to all of the doubts and fears flooding my mind. In that moment, I made a choice. I chose to stand up for everything I believe in and work for. I chose to stand up for what I teach when I tell thousands of people that *if you can see it and you believe it and you are willing to do whatever it takes to get it, then you can achieve it.* I chose to stand up to the fear and the doubt that had crept into my mind. I chose to believe in myself and the work that I do. And then I replied, "Yes, Stan, I can help you." And that's exactly what I did.

I created a mental game plan for Stan, and he embraced it. He committed to it, working at it faithfully until race day. On June 6, 2015, he was mentally ready. He ran some good miles and some not-so-good miles. He struggled. He hurt. He broke down. At times, he was reduced to tears. He stood up. He kept going. He completed the race. He ran 100 miles in 25 hours and 21 minutes, finishing 51st out of 250 competitors. And now, without any hesitation, I confidently and with everything I believe in tell you that I have no doubt... **the mind leads the body**. We are capable as human beings of doing so much more than we think we can. It is our fears, and ultimately our mind, that quit on us first. But know this. You **CAN** train the mind the same way you train the body. You **CAN** build a mindset for success, so let's get going.

THE FEAR ROADBLOCK

One of the biggest barriers to success is FEAR. I am referring to fear of making mistakes, fear of failure, fear of not being good enough, fear of not getting what you want, or not getting to where you want to be, fear of what people think, or of how you will be judged. FEAR, FEAR, FEAR!!!

It is this underlying fear that becomes the ultimate success killer. Think for a moment about how fear gets the best of you as an athlete on the ice, on the court or on the playing field. As an adult, a professional or a parent, consider how fear holds you back at work, at home, in your relationships or with your children. As a coach, look at how fear impacts your coaching decisions, player recruitment, team culture or players' performance. As a teacher, how does fear impact your work, your dealings with parents and administration, and how does fear within your students impact their learning? Think about what you fear in your life today that is holding you back from moving forward or developing and performing to your peak level of potential. Ask yourself: *What am I afraid of?*

A new client, we'll call him Mike, told me his agent suggested he give me a call. Mike was a strong and skilled hockey player who was a top round National Hockey League (NHL) draft pick. He had reasonable success in his first couple of seasons at the NHL level before being traded. Now part of a higher ranked team, he didn't quite crack the lineup out of training camp. He was signed on a two-way contract, and was assigned to the affiliate team in the American Hockey League (AHL), otherwise known as the farm team. This was a devastating blow. Mike certainly did not get what he had wanted, especially having lived the difference between the AHL and NHL lifestyles which, he explained, was quite drastic. He went from flying high in private planes with gourmet food and more money than he had ever seen, back to long bus rides and a much lower level salary in comparison. He was devastated.

One morning, early in the season, Mike's phone rang; it was the call he had been waiting for. The voice on the other end said, "Pack your bags and be ready to go. We need you tonight." With an injured player on the main team, here was his chance to get back into the NHL lineup.

"I'll be ready," Mike replied. He hung up the phone and started running through his house yelling, "They called! They called! I am going back up tonight!"

It was an incredible moment full of elation, but a moment was all it was. It didn't last long as the excitement quickly turned to fear when a flood of thoughts started rushing through Mike's head. *I need to show them that I deserve to be there. I had better be great tonight. I had better not mess up. I need to have the game of my life. I can't give them any reason to send me back down! I don't want to go back down.* He had wanted so badly to stay up with the NHL team, and was so determined to prove himself to the coach, that his fear of not playing well enough to keep his spot began to take over his mind. It generated so much pressure and anxiety that it seemed virtually impossible to play a good game. But off he went. His bags were packed and he was ready to go. Unfortunately, some extra emotional baggage filled with fear and anxiety made the trip with him.

As he told me his story, Mike recounted how good it felt to walk back into an NHL arena to play, but once again, that feeling was fleeting. His nerves were getting the best of him. Mike began to feel sick to his stomach and started throwing up before the game. He splashed some cold water on his face, took a swig of Gatorade, pulled himself together, and out he went. He walked out of the dressing room, down the hall and toward the ice. He could hear the hum of the crowd. It was game time. Mike was shaky in warm-up, hoping that his nerves would soon calm down. The buzzer sounded and sent a shrill down his spine. He headed toward the bench and sat down with the team. Trying to get motivated, he continued thinking that he was there to prove himself, to show the coach, and to be great. Yet it was hard to breathe, he told me. "All I kept saying in my mind was *Don't f#$k this up!!*"

You want to take a guess at how his first shift went? He made a bad pass and things spiraled downward from there. On the bench, he beat himself up for making that first mistake. Mike consumed himself with worry about being sent back down. His next shift was not great either. All the while, his fear and anxiety continued to rise while his confidence continued to plummet. Needless to say, Mike did not have a very good game that night. And then it happened: the thing he feared the most and so desperately wanted to avoid was exactly what he had created. Only ten minutes after the game ended, he was sent back down to the farm team.

Mike didn't realize it at the time, of course, but there is no doubt about what it was that derailed his hopes of rejoining the team. It was his mindset. He had made a common mistake. He believed that his self-talk was a way of pushing him harder to get what he wanted. The truth is, it was a setup for failure right from the start. There was no way that Mike was in the right headspace to allow himself to play to his potential. In order to create his desired success, he would have needed to be fully focused on the game, with no distractions. Instead, his focus was on everything but the actual game: his fears, not messing up, the need to prove himself, what the coach was thinking, the AHL versus the NHL, and so on. His thoughts were everywhere except where they really needed to be. If only Mike had been aware of how his thinking was hurting him, perhaps the game would have played out differently. But he didn't know. This brings me to the first thing we all need in order to begin gaining strength, generating change, and inspiring personal greatness from within: *awareness*.

BECOMING AWARE

Self-awareness is all about having a clear and accurate understanding of knowledge and insight into one's own thoughts, feelings, behaviours, desires, motives, actions and character. A key component of emotional intelligence, it allows us to make changes in our beliefs and behaviours, leading to growth, change, and ultimately, success. First off, we need to be aware of how we think. Our thinking is so powerful. It is our thinking that becomes the underlying force driving us into action. To illustrate this point, consider the following statement. These words are key to my understanding of the athletes and other people I work with, and the key that helps me unlock major barriers holding people back.

Our thoughts drive our feelings, which then result in our behaviours and our actions, of which there are consequences—good or bad.

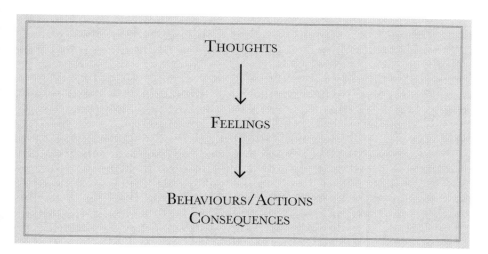

THOUGHTS

↓

FEELINGS

↓

BEHAVIOURS/ACTIONS
CONSEQUENCES

Our thoughts are behind everything we do. They form the way we see and interpret the world around us. The problem is that the majority of our thinking patterns have become somewhat automatic; they have been developed from childhood and the experiences we have had since. Our thoughts are firing all of the time, but we are rarely aware and fully conscious of them. It is believed that, on average, a person has between 50,000 to 80,000 thoughts a day. Are you aware of those tens of thousands of thoughts flying through your head? How about the approximate 2,000 to 4,000 thoughts you have in one hour? Or the approximate 35 to 48 thoughts in your mind every minute? Those are a lot of thoughts to keep track of.

I always say that every person wears his or her own set of shades. We each walk around the world seeing and interpreting through our own particular vision and way of thinking. Here's where the real problem comes in: people mess up their thinking all the time. Yet, it is this thinking that generates our emotional response, which is typically when we first become aware. Interestingly, we are very well aware of how we are feeling, be it angry, happy, sad, nervous or otherwise. And it is our emotional state that dictates our behavioural responses, resulting in either positive or negative consequences.

Let's take Mike's story from above. His thoughts were intense and fearful. They were not helping him to be a great hockey player—and were in fact hindering him—but Mike wasn't aware of his thoughts at the time. Based on his *thoughts*, he was quite understandably feeling highly anxious. All of those thoughts were running through his head without him thinking or analyzing what he was thinking, yet he only became aware at the *feelings* level. He certainly knew how he was feeling; he was tuned into how nervous and anxious he was. Then, his emotional state resulted in an increased heart rate, muscle tension, and vomiting, leading to his on-ice *behaviours* which were tight, tense and hesitant. The *consequences* of playing in that state were clear.

It is essential to become aware of our thinking and determine whether it is helping us or hurting us. Fear stems from fearful thinking or the interpretation that something is scary, could be scary, or could turn out badly. The biggest problem is that our bodies can't tell the difference between real danger and perceived danger. If we send ourselves a message of danger, real or not, our bodies will react accordingly. Now, that might help you if you were in a real danger situation, but it does not help when it comes to your performance, whether it is in sport, at work, at school, or in everyday life. We must challenge and replace that fearful thinking with a more powerful and productive thought process that can help move us forward and not keep us stuck. It is a mindset thing. The right mindset—one that knows the difference between real and perceived danger in a fearful or high pressure situation—is essential to building success. So start to become aware!

As you read on, I will give you what I call Target Thoughts, along with Strategies, Taglines, Exercises and Quotes. Use the Target Thoughts to challenge old thinking and build a more productive mindset, paying special attention when you are faced with adversity. Incorporate the Strategies and Exercises to help gain awareness and produce better behaviours and outcomes. Say the Taglines to reinforce the lessons you learn here. And read the Quotes to inspire you on your road to greatness.

Use the 3 R's strategy below to recognize and re-direct your attention away from unproductive thinking patterns.

STRATEGY: THE 3 R'S - RECOGNIZE, REGROUP, REFOCUS

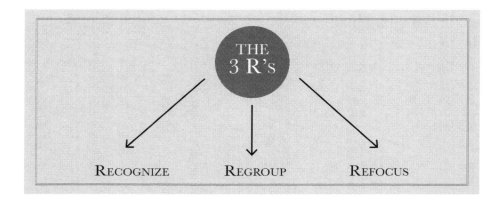

Step 1, R1 - RECOGNIZE

When you are nervous, anxious or afraid, ask yourself, *What am I thinking?* This question will help you become aware of the thoughts, self-talk and messages that are driving you.

Step 2, R2 - REGROUP

Remind yourself that this type of fearful thinking does not help you. It only hurts you.

Step 3, R3 - REFOCUS

Refocus yourself on new thinking and behaviours (which you will continue to learn about throughout this book) that will help you and be productive for you.

We all get nervous and scared. That anxious feeling is a normal and natural human emotion. Growth, change and putting yourself out there is scary. Failure, rejection, loss, and pain are scary. **Moving forward is not about the absence of fear altogether. Rather, it is about recognizing your fears and becoming fearless in your approach to facing them.**

Whatever it is you are afraid of, you must face it, figure out how to deal with it and how to prepare for it. Figure out how to stand back up when you get knocked down, because everyone will get knocked down. The most important point, though, is how you choose to *think* about the situation and your fear, because your thinking will drive how you are going to respond to it. Will you stay down, or will you get back up? And consider this: Do you even allow yourself the opportunity to face the initial fear and move forward into those situations that put you at risk? Or do you just shy away from them instead?

If you don't allow yourself to be in anxiety-provoking situations, you can't grow, improve or change. These scary situations are opportunities because they are the ones that eventually allow you to learn. Facing things, trying things, and standing up one more time than you have been knocked down is what allows people to grow and develop as athletes, professionals, students, coaches, teachers and individuals. Stop being afraid to face whatever it is you fear! Growth develops outside of comfort zones, so get prepared and do it anyway!

PREPARE THEN PROCEED

Let's get real here. My friend Stan did not welcome the vomiting, pain and vicious leg cramping he suffered in his first 60-mile race. It was pain that made it impossible for him to even stand up at times, never mind run. It was in many ways a dreadful experience that instilled fear in him, especially knowing how much worse it could be in the 100-mile race. But Stan recognized that this pain was all part and parcel of running the race; it came with the territory. He did not, however, spend his time caught up in thoughts of how horrible the experience was. Instead, I worked with Stan to help him become fearless in his approach going forward. We did this by creating a plan for adversity—a clear plan of action to deal with the pain, the leg cramping and the vomiting he experienced.

By the time he ran the next race, Stan had practiced step-by-step how he was going to approach each one of those scenarios. We did this work so that when his mind was weak, he wouldn't have to let the thoughts of giving up take over. Instead, he would be able to think in terms of individual steps toward a goal. He was prepared to meet adversity by knowing, and thinking, *This is what I need to do now.* This plan helped guide him into the action of moving forward instead of staying trapped in his fear. Because Stan was prepared to face his fear, he did not allow fear to take over.

You, too, can build a more productive thought process by learning to speak a new language when you talk yourself through fear and adversity. Positive and productive self-talk has immense power, so it's time to start using it.

Target Thought: *I can be scared and do it anyway.*

Combine the strategy below with the target thought above to further help alleviate some of the fear by having a back-up plan.

Strategy: If/Then - Replace *What if?* with *If then*

If you are worried about something, create a plan to deal with it instead of staying entangled in your fears. I remember the first time I began speaking in front of large groups. I was nervous because I wanted my speech to run smoothly and to positively impact my audience. But instead of fixating on all the things that could go wrong, I started to focus on the things that I could do to help it go right. I prepared! I practiced and practiced and practiced. I also created a plan just in case something did go wrong. **If** I was to mess up, **then** I had a plan for what I would do. As a result of my preparation however, nothing went wrong. Following that talk, I delivered many, many more successful talks. But then one day, it happened.

I was speaking to all of the coaches and parents at the Toronto Mets Baseball Organization, which is a high level baseball club for youth between the ages of 14 and 18. The talk was going well, until I got distracted. A new thought came into my head about something I wanted to add to my speech and share with the group. While I was speaking, I was thinking, *How am I going to fit this in?* And suddenly, I lost my train of thought. I forgot about what I was saying and what was supposed to come next. It had never happened to me before, but there it was. I froze for a few seconds, although those seconds felt a lot longer. And then it hit me. I had an If/Then plan that I had devised long ago, in case I tripped up during a speech.

My plan was to refuse to allow my mistake to take hold of my mind. Instead, I called it right out and made a joke about it and about myself. Right there in front of the whole audience, I laughed at myself, and I got a chuckle from them in return. I showed everyone that despite the fact that I do public speaking so often, I still mess up sometimes, and the audience could relate. It was a great moment because not only did it help me regroup and refocus, but it also showed everyone that I am human. It became okay to not be perfect, and at the same time, it allowed me to get myself back on track. The talk as a whole ended up being a hit, and I was flattered by the positive feedback people shared with me afterward. My backup plan worked. It also reminded me that most of what people worry about doesn't actually come true, so we need to stop getting caught up in worrying so much. Instead, prepare yourself and have the If/Then plan in your back pocket if necessary. From there, you are good to go.

Target Thought: *Most of what we worry about doesn't actually come true.*

Consider some of the most successful people you know. I bet they all have a sense of fearlessness and the ability to risk, try, fall, stand up and try again. I bet they have the wherewithal to hang in there, no matter what they have had to face. I trust they have the strength to work hard and do whatever it takes to keep moving forward to get to where they want to be. That's how success is achieved.

Think for a minute about the basketball icon Michael Jordan who, at 15 years old, was cut from his high school basketball team. Most of us just see the accomplished athlete that Michael Jordan is today, but let's consider how that early failure impacted him and his eventual success. The fact is, when Michael Jordan was 15, there were enough other guys out there who were more desirable players to fill the team than he was. So what did he do about it?

If you are a young athlete right now (or the parent of an athlete whose confidence is waning because others are better players) and you didn't make that team you wanted, or you did make it but are not getting the playing time, or you are too small, or someone beat you, or your coach is on you all the time, or you are facing some other challenge that is getting you down, how are you choosing to think about it? Is it disappointing? Yes, of course it is. But where are you choosing to put your focus? Do you focus on the fact that you are not where you want to be right now and on all of the things that are not working for you? Do you decide that you suck and that you are not good enough to compete? Or, do you use your situation to drive you harder? Do you believe that you CAN get there if you keep working? Do you understand that there is still a long way to go and that there is no way to determine at 15 years old how far you can get, if only you can hang in there? Do you take the time to learn and recognize that growth and development occur at different times and stages for different people? Know this: Where you choose to direct your thinking determines how you do or do not move forward.

Because Michael Jordan did not make his high school team, he woke up to practice his game every day before school. He used his experience to drive him harder. He did not have the advantage of money or trainers to make him better. He just worked hard. By doing so, he became prepared. He never gave up, and he got better. He failed, and he got back up. That is how Michael Jordan became what and who he is today. Don't forget his story when you are feeling down in the dumps because things are not going your way.

"I've failed over and over again in my life, and that's why I succeed." – **Michael Jordan**

So, what is it really that makes someone successful? Success comes from the ability to recognize thoughts and fears, be willing to face them and become fearless in the approach to dealing with them.

From there, you need the work ethic, passion, and ability to keep moving forward in pursuit of your goals and dreams, no matter what adversity you face along the way. If you realize that you can train your mind in the same way you train your body, you will be able to work at and embrace these concepts, live them, and model that type of mindset for those around you.

CHAPTER 2

I'M JUST NOT GOOD ENOUGH

TALENT VERSUS MENTAL TOUGHNESS

Amy was a very talented 15-year-old volleyball player, often described as a "natural". But Amy was sad and usually stressed out, despite the overall success she had achieved over the years on the court. She had gotten used to being the best based on her natural talent, and she grew up having that notion reinforced by all those around her. Amy continued to do the things that were working well for her so she could keep shining on the court. The problem was, she would stay away from doing anything she was not good at, or that could potentially expose signs of weakness.

As Amy grew, she became driven by the need for perfection. When she fell short, she was terribly hard on herself. She identified her shortcomings as a sign of weakness, and weakness was the one thing she desperately needed to avoid. Consequently, Amy started judging every move and shot she made. Her judgmental thinking was her way of taking mental inventory with respect to how she was doing. She judged herself before, during and after her games. She would tell herself that she was either better or worse than the other players. Amy would think, *I was the best out there today* or *I completely sucked; I had a great game* or *I was absolutely terrible.* Mistakes, weakness and loss all meant the same thing to her: *I am not good enough. What will people think?*

Standing at 5'10" at the age of 15 also became unacceptable to her. She compared her height to that of the other girls, especially those over six feet tall. Amy became an emotional mess both on and off the court and began to be recognized mostly for her lack of emotional control, which in turn began jeopardizing her chances to advance from the amateur to the professional level.

MASTERING YOUR MINDSET

What went wrong? Amy supposedly had it all, from her desire to be the best, to her natural talent. What happened? Carol Dweck, a world-renowned research psychologist in the areas of achievement and success, helps us to understand this phenomenon through her work on mindset. Dweck discovered two types of mindsets that we should all be aware of: the growth mindset and the fixed mindset. The fixed mindset is characterized by thoughts and beliefs that our basic traits, such as talent and intelligence, are fixed. People with this mindset believe there is nothing much they can do to change or improve upon who, what, and how they are. These people tend to stay away from exposing weaknesses and tend to fear failure. The growth mindset, on the other hand, teaches that we can improve those basic qualities if we are willing to keep working at them. People with this mindset are willing to try new things, face failure, try again, learn from their mistakes, and keep working until they figure it out. They tend to have a love for learning and an ability to develop a sense of grit and resilience, which are integral to achieving success.

Not surprisingly, most people who have attained great success come from the perspective of the growth mindset. This fact does not mean that people with the fixed mindset are any less driven toward success than those with the growth mindset. They are. Most people in general want to have a positive self-image and achieve success in their lives. The difference, however, is their approach to it.

It's their thinking and mindset that translates to their behaviours and actions.

Let's get back to volleyball player Amy for a moment. She was extremely driven to succeed, but her thinking and approach came from the perspective of the fixed mindset. Amy had learned early on that she had a natural gift, and she relied upon that gift to succeed. She stayed away from challenges whenever possible, as she feared they would make her look bad. She turned a blind eye to any form of critical feedback, as it represented a sign of weakness to her, and she was threatened by the success of others, fearing that she would not be considered to be the best.

As Amy progressed through her sport, this mindset began to destroy her. If only Amy could have viewed challenge as opportunity, critical feedback as a chance to work on what she needed to improve, and others' success as a form of inspiration. Perhaps then she could have channeled her energy and efforts into facing and growing from challenges, overcoming obstacles, improving, and learning from those around her, to become the best that she could potentially be. Most importantly, she could have enjoyed her journey along the way. It was the fixed mindset that prevented her from doing any of those things and ultimately stopped her from growing. Had she employed a growth mindset, who knows where she might have ended up. Yet the barriers to success that she created chained her down and prevented her from breaking free.

Let me now throw out the name J.K. Rowling, author of the famous Harry Potter series, which has become one of history's most popular book series and film franchises. Rowling, who had a love for writing, came from humble beginnings and went on to face considerable adversity. In her teens, Rowling lost her mother, and she went on to have a short-lived marriage that blew up, leaving her a single mother, jobless and broke. But she had an idea. She had a passion. Despite her circumstances, she had a belief that she could to do something to make a better life for herself and for her daughter.

In 1990, Rowling began to write her first book, *Harry Potter and the Philosopher's Stone*, which, believe it or not, was rejected by several publishers. But she didn't give up. She kept working. She believed in something bigger and better than where she was at in her life, and finally one day, her book got picked up. It was bought for approximately $4,000. By the year 2000, she had written the first three *Harry Potter* books which earned $480 million, quite a dramatic increase. Today, Rowling is one of the most successful authors of our time, having achieved billionaire status from her books. She has since given up this super elite status, due to her charitable donations, and taken herself out of billionaire net worth.

I guess settling for multi-millionaire status, giving back, and being an amazing person is not so bad! J.K. Rowling did alright after all. Most importantly, she moved forward because of the growth mindset. She explains it like this: "I was set free because my greatest fear had been realized and I still had a daughter that I adored, and I had an old typewriter and a big idea. And so rock bottom became a solid foundation on which I rebuilt my life."

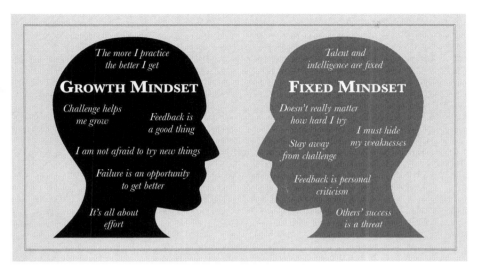

The more I practice
the better I get

GROWTH MINDSET

Challenge helps
me grow

Feedback is
a good thing

I am not afraid to try new things

Failure is an opportunity
to get better

It's all about
effort

Talent and
intelligence are fixed

FIXED MINDSET

Doesn't really matter
how hard I try

I must hide
my weaknesses

Stay away
from challenge

Feedback is personal
criticism

Others' success
is a threat

WHY TALENT IS OVERRATED

Are some people naturally gifted and better at some things than others? Do we all have different strengths and weaknesses? Are some more naturally inclined to the growth mindset versus the fixed mindset? The answer to all of these questions is yes. And to that I say **so what?!** Sure, it is wonderful to be blessed with intelligence, size, strength, athleticism, leadership abilities, business sense, artistic style, or any other special ability, but research shows that natural talent only accounts for approximately 30% of someone's long-term success. You could have all of the natural talent in the world, but if you don't have the right mindset, the work ethic and the ability to persevere when things go wrong, then, in my opinion, you have nothing.

Alternately, you may not be naturally gifted in one area or another, but if you have the drive and determination of a lion, there will be no stopping you. If you believe only in the power of your talents, or if you judge yourself by where you are today, it will be very difficult to progress. You don't have to settle for what you've got or the status quo. The mind is a muscle. If you work it, you can grow it.

WHAT IS MENTAL TOUGHNESS?

The term *mental toughness* gets thrown around all the time. While it can refer to many different attributes, what is it exactly? My simple definition of mental toughness is having a strong and powerful mind to deal with any and all of the demands of doing what you do. From there, it is about having the passion and persistence to keep moving forward no matter what it is you may be faced with on any given day. Famous research psychologist Angela Duckworth refers to this characteristic as *grit*.

Duckworth's groundbreaking research from the University of Pennsylvania found that grit, which she defines as having the passion and perseverance for long-term goals, is essential to high-level achievement. Duckworth took her studies regarding predictors of performance in high-level achievers and success to West Point Military Academy in the United States. She studied freshman students, entering their first seven-week Beast Barracks summer training program. This program is designed to turn civilians into military cadets. True to its name, Beast Barracks is a nasty place, specifically engineered to push cadets to their limits, both physically and mentally. It is also interesting to note that admission into West Point itself is extraordinarily competitive, with many rigorous enrollment criteria such as class ranking, physical aptitude, leadership abilities, and SAT scores, along with a required nomination from a member of Congress or from the Department of the Army. Despite the extensive admission process, there is still a significant dropout rate during that first summer of training.

Duckworth and her research team set out to see if they could determine the greatest predictive factor contributing to success over the course of the summer training. They tested the cadets on their second and third days into the program, looking at their intelligence, leadership skills, physical strength, conditioning, stamina, grit and overall mental toughness, and then off they went. Due to the rugged physical demands of the training program, many would predict that size, strength and physical conditioning would be fundamental to the success of making it through the training program. However, the results were surprising. They showed that it wasn't size, strength or natural talents that propelled people toward success, but rather their levels of mental toughness. In fact, those who scored higher on their levels of grit were found to be 60% more likely to complete the training program.

Duckworth and her team also took their studies outside the realm of physical size and strength by testing to see if there was a correlation between grit and Grade Point Average (GPA) among undergraduate students at an elite university in the U.S. Who do you think had the higher GPAs? Was it those who were naturally intellectually gifted, or those with the highest levels of mental toughness, grit and passion? I think you know where this is going; those gritty students outperformed their less gritty counterparts and achieved the higher overall GPA.

Let's look at some of my own research analysis. I find it intriguing that Martin St. Louis, Tyler Johnson, Tyler Bozak and Chris Kunitz have something very interesting in common. Yes, they are all past or present NHL players, but did you know that they were all undrafted players? In other words, when draft day came along, a highly anticipated day for these athletes, their names were NOT called. They sat hour after hour, round after round, hoping, waiting, anticipating, and watching other guys they played with getting called, but they never heard their own names. There is no doubt that this experience was heartbreaking! Devastating! The point, however, is that they did not allow heartbreak or devastation to stop them. They kept going, kept working and stayed determined. And look what happened. Not only did they get to where they wanted to be, but they became impact players at the NHL level.

Have you heard of Alexandre Daigle, A.J. Thelen or Jesse Niinimäki? You may not be as familiar with these names. Well, let me tell you what they have in common. They were all first round NHL draft picks with all the natural talent in the world. They dominated their Minor and Junior hockey careers. They were top notch talent, first round picks. Yet they are unfamiliar to most people. Get this: Alexandre Daigle was not only a first round pick, but he also happened to be the first overall pick. The best of the best! Sadly, he is now considered to be one of the biggest draft busts in NHL history. When it came time to play in the NHL, he simply couldn't cut it and did not survive at the NHL level.

How about you football fans? Do you know that Tom Brady was a very late draft pick and that six other quarterbacks were chosen before he was? He is now the only quarterback in National Football League (NFL) history to have won five Super Bowl championships, and he is the only player to have been awarded Super Bowl MVP (Most Valuable Player) four times. He is considered to be the greatest steal in NFL draft history. Alternately, let's look at Johnny Manziel, also referred to as "Johnny Football". This guy was considered to be a superstar and was the 22nd overall pick by the Cleveland Browns in the 2014 NFL draft. After being nationally recruited out of high school, breaking numerous records, winning multiple awards while playing in the NCAA and being the first freshman ever to win the Heisman Trophy, Manziel was released from the Browns at the end of the 2015 season, and was unable to get picked up by another team. So, consider the following quote, uttered by high school basketball coach Tim Notke and made famous by pro basketball player Kevin Durant.

"Hard work beats talent when talent isn't working hard." – **Tim Notke, Basketball Coach**

And here's another great line that makes the same point.

"Genius is 1% inspiration (talent) and 99% perspiration (hard work)." – **Thomas Edison**

When you stop to think about it, this is all great news. Why? Because while we can't change our parents or the genes we were born with, we **CAN** develop our grit, mental toughness and mindset. With practice and persistence, we can build the muscles of the mind. And since mindset is one of the biggest contributing factors to success, then it's time we start building the growth mindset and the right type of thinking. Make today the day you start working on becoming GREAT! Dream big, work hard and don't give up.

I don't care who you are, where you are now, or what your starting point is. I don't care if you are the best or the worst athlete, professional, corporate executive, coach, teacher, parent, or whatever it is you do right now; if you are willing to think right and work at it, you **will** get better. If you are willing to face your fears and weaknesses, embrace your failure and grow from it and try again, you will improve. In fact, you have no idea just how far you can get if you have the right approach. When we stop believing, we stop trying. That's the moment when we give up on ourselves. So, recognize that you do have a choice. Don't be afraid to follow your passions. Strive for excellence in whatever you do, or want to do. Just get ready to take that first step forward, which will lead you to another step, and so on, and so on. It's all about stamina. Keep your mind strong and your effort level high, especially in times of slow progress, difficulty, failure, and adversity.

Target Thought: *The more I continuously work at anything, the better I will get.*

PUT AWAY THE CRYSTAL BALL

Today is an important day as you begin to work on building that powerful and productive mindset. Not yesterday, not tomorrow, but today. Everything starts today. Yesterday is behind us. It is a memory that we can simply use to learn from today. Tomorrow is not yet here, so don't waste your time in the present worrying about the possibilities of it. Today is where you are, and if you don't like where you are, then do something about it—today!

The fact is, your current state does not tell me anything about where you will be in the future. Focusing on the journey is what counts, not the destination. What you decide to do today and how you choose to think right now, in this moment, will lead you to where you are going. Do you worry that you are not big enough, not smart enough, not fast enough? Stop drawing conclusions about yourself just because you are not where you want to be at this point in time. You cannot predict the future. Unless you have some magical powers that I don't know about, stop allowing your mind to speculate (that's the *thinking*) that you can't get there. Doing so simply leads to bad feelings (that's the *emotion*) and most likely giving up (that's the *behaviour*). It is almost impossible to persevere if you decide that you are not good enough today. Put away the crystal ball. It is sabotaging your success.

Today is the day you need to say: *I will strive for greatness and I will not be afraid to fail.* Your job is to work to keep getting better. There's a long way to go. If you are prepared to do the right things and focus on the right things, let's see where you can get to, one step at a time. Patience, passion, perseverance—that's what we are going for.

Let me tell you a story about a boy named Noah who started playing hockey at the age of five. He was a pretty determined little guy who seemed to love the game from a very young age. He was only three years old the first time he stood up on skates using a little training aid to help him balance and stand. For a few seconds, Noah stood and didn't move. His eyes wandered around the rink, watching the kids who had been taking lessons for some time. Some of them were fortunate enough to have a plastic hockey stick and ball to hit and chase around the rink. Well, Noah's eyes lit up when he saw that, and he locked them on those kids. He looked at his training aid and then back at those young aspiring hockey players. He did this a few times, back and forth. And then he pushed away the aid and started moving. He took baby steps. Lots of them. It took him almost the entire class to reach the instructor carrying the sticks, but he did it. He finally got there, picked up a stick and away he went. He didn't care how many times he fell down, what he looked like, or what others were thinking. He was three years old and so excited to have that stick in his hand. Sometimes all we need is to get back to that inner child inside of us and just go for it.

After learning how to skate, Noah moved on to playing with his first hockey team. A few years later, at the age of eight, he moved up to AAA, which is the most competitive level in minor hockey. The only problem was that Noah was a little guy, and being small is not looked upon favourably in the world of competitive hockey. He got very used to being referred to as *Little Noah* and hearing, "You're too small." But he never really took it to heart—until the day he got cut from his team because body checking was starting the following season. He was ten years old at the time, and getting cut was quite a blow. He was let go of a team he loved. He was forced to stop playing with his friends, and he had to watch as they secured a spot on the team he was no longer part of. Even worse, his defense partner from the team was one of his best friends, and the coach's son. The coach, a close family friend as well, was the one who made the cut. Devastated, Noah's family had no choice but to move on so Noah could continue to play the game he loved.

It was a real heartbreak at a young age, but Noah managed to make another AAA team and he continued to play. In time, he learned to adjust and he made new friends. Year after year, however, the concern about his size continued to grow, and he struggled to make a roster every season. Noah hung in there, continued to work and learned how to play a smart game in order to make up for his lack of size. He continued to forge ahead despite being told he would be at the bottom of the lineup for ice time because of his limited size and strength. And yet somehow, every year, Noah climbed his way up the lineup and earned his ice time as well as some respect from his coaches. Fast forward a number of years to his Minor Midget year, the draft year for the Ontario Hockey League (OHL). He was 15 years old and began the season at 5'3" and 125 pounds, about 6 to 8 inches smaller and 40 to 60 pounds lighter than his average teammate or opponent. Nonetheless, he continued to play his game and focus on his goals.

Noah learned at a young age not to allow anyone to break his spirit or stop him from playing the game he loved. And then it happened. Little Noah finally had a growth spurt. He grew seven inches over the course of that year. While he was still considered undersized at only 145 pounds, Noah was drafted to the OHL.

Noah and his family didn't realize it at the time, but being cut from his team at age ten was one of the greatest things that could have happened to him. It taught him never to allow anyone to break him. It also opened new doors, eventually landing him on a team where he had a coach who recognized and appreciated the skills that Noah brought to the game. This coach was willing to develop Noah into the player he became. And it all happened because his closest family friend at the time broke his heart. Five years earlier, if Noah had bought into the belief that he wasn't good enough, big enough, or strong enough, like everyone had told him, he never would have gotten to where he is today—drafted to the OHL and currently in the U.S. playing prep hockey on a scholarship while attending a highly reputable academic school program as he pursues his goal to play in the NCAA.

It is amazing how when one door closes, another opens; you might just not know it at the time. I certainly didn't, as that Little Noah, who is not to so little anymore, happens to be my son. The coach who cut Noah five years earlier continued coaching that team until just before their Minor Midget season. Then, just before the most important year in minor hockey, the draft year, the organization let go of both him and his son, leaving them scrambling at the last minute to make a new team. Often in life, things do seem to come full circle. You just have to have the courage and strength to stay the course, because what happens today is not a predictor of the future.

The fact is, **greatness takes time**—regardless of whether you have natural talent or not. I know this is a difficult pill to swallow sometimes, especially in our day and age where instant gratification is literally at our fingertips. We live in a fast-paced world of technology where advances are being made every day, a world where everyone is attached to their phones, and pretty much anything you need is just a click or two away. Need a ride? Download Uber. Want to show the world what you are doing? Instagram, Facebook or Snapchat it. Hungry? Uber Eats delivers right to your door. Have something to say? Tweet it. Like someone? Swipe right. It is all incredible technology but beware: there is a cost. With all of the benefits, there is a downside. We have lost the appreciation for the process and the sense of waiting and working for what we want. As parents, leaders, coaches, and teachers, we are losing the opportunities to be able to teach our children how to put in the necessary time. One thing has not changed however: success takes time. Building healthy and productive relationships takes time. Greatness takes time. Please give yourself that reminder today and every day. Stay the course and put away the crystal ball.

Articulation Exercise: Brainstorm your passions and desires.

Think about what you would really want to achieve in your life if you could eliminate your fears, and then write it down. Articulating your true aspirations in the absence of fear will help to provide insight and clarity and allow you to begin to see how fear has been holding you back.

CHAPTER 3

LEADING WITH CONFIDENCE

DO YOU BELIEVE?

Let me circle back to that thinking I refer to in Chapter 1 and ask you a question: Do you believe? Do you believe in yourself? Do you believe in your ability to get to where you want to be? If so, how much do you believe? The strength of your belief in yourself and your ability to do what you have to do, or to get to where you want to be, is another essential component to success. Belief in yourself is the fundamental concept in defining confidence. Successful athletes, entrepreneurs, professionals, musicians, artists and people in general do what they do with confidence. They believe that, irrespective of their successes or failures to date, they **CAN** get to where they want to be.

Belief in oneself is a thought process that is commonly held by those who fall under the growth mindset. Believing in yourself generates a sense of confidence resulting in positive behaviours and actions such as the ability to persevere. Disbelief is also a thought process, but one that is typically associated with the fixed mindset. A lack of belief in yourself generates a lack of confidence, negative emotions and, ultimately, negative behaviours and actions such as making excuses, giving up, or not trying.

THOUGHT	EMOTION	BEHAVIOUR
I can do it	Confident	Perseverance
I will never get there	Unconfident	Self doubt; give up

Successful people behave with confidence. Successful athletes perform with confidence. Successful entrepreneurs carry themselves with confidence. Successful teachers and coaches teach with confidence and instill confidence in their students and athletes. It is difficult to be great at anything if you don't first believe, and if you don't bring a high level of confidence to what you do.

"I told myself I was the greatest, even before I knew I was." Do you know who said that? It was Muhammed Ali, one of the greatest boxers of all time. And do you know why he said that? He figured that if he kept saying it over and over again, he would not only convince himself but also the rest of the world that it was true. And that is exactly what he did. He believed it, and then he became it. He embodied the characteristics of a champion and then developed into one.

> *"I told myself I was the greatest, even before I knew I was."* **– Muhammed Ali, Boxer**

Target Thought: *Why can't I?*

Far too often, people get caught up in judging themselves, robbing themselves of confidence. They also look around and compare themselves to others who are better than they are, or beat themselves down when they fall short of their own expectations. People can get so busy reacting and responding to what is happening, or what has happened to them, and then draw conclusions based on those situations. Doing any or all of these things causes confidence to go up and down like a yo-yo based on how life or performance is going on any given day. The thinking and interpretations involved not only generate anxiety and negative feelings, but also make it impossible to carry oneself with consistent confidence. One of the big mistakes people make with their thinking is getting caught up in mind-reading. You get yourself into trouble when you are either thinking about what others are thinking, jumping to conclusions, or making generalizations based on one particular situation or interaction. All of these actions trap people in unproductive thinking.

I also like to categorize thinking into the three different tenses: past, present and future. Doing so helps to identify ways that people sabotage themselves with their thinking patterns. When it comes to performance, we need to be in the here and now—the present. It is in the present where one can attain peak level performance on or off the playing field. Spending your time thinking in the past, or forecasting the future, is neither helpful nor productive when it comes to performance as well as confidence.

PAST ←——————→ PRESENT ←——————→ FUTURE

THINK IN THE PRESENT

Past thinking often involves a lot of *shoulds* and *should haves*. A perfect example of past thinking is ruminating about your last mistake. When you focus on what you could have or should have done better, you are criticizing yourself for something you didn't do well. Now, I don't know about you, but I certainly don't have any special powers to send me back in time and change the past. So, if you stay stuck in that type of thinking, the only thing you'll be left with is a bad feeling. When I notice my athletes directing their attention to the past when competing, especially when it is their mistakes they are focusing on, I tell them I am going to give them my imaginary whip. When they are done beating themselves up, they can give it back, because that's about all they are going to get from staying stuck in that place.

On the other hand, when people are lost in worrying about the future, they tend to do a lot of *what if* thinking, which leads to catastrophizing. Again, if you don't have magical powers or fortune telling abilities, then why are you spending your time building problems that don't even exist yet? So often my clients ask me, *What if I mess up?* Or, *I want this so badly, what if I don't make it?* Well, you can't predict the future and you can't fix a problem that is not even real yet. Consequently, the only outcome this type of thinking produces is nerves and anxiety. It's hard to be confident and great at something when you are being driven by anxiety, worry and fear of failure.

When you are in performance mode, your job is to be 100% focused in the present moment. If you are feeling bad, it is a good indicator that you are caught up in the past. If you are feeling anxious, then you are most likely focused on the future. You need to recognize when this forward or backward thinking is happening and tell yourself to **STOP!** Get yourself out of the past and/or future, so you can focus on the present.

Use the following strategy to stop ineffective thinking and get yourself out of a negative emotional state.

Strategy: Thought Stopping

Recognize your unproductive thinking and yell **STOP!** If there are people around then repeat the word silently over and over in your head. You might also imagine yourself running into a giant red stop sign. If you are an athlete, you might imagine the referee blowing the whistle and stopping the play. However it is that you choose to do it, practice stopping those thoughts that are getting you into trouble and undermining your confidence and performance.

Your past experiences, both good and bad, are just that—past. While you can't change them, they can provide you with valuable information in the present. Take those experiences and bring them into the present and learn from them TODAY. Next, get yourself out of the future. You have no crystal ball, so put the idea of it away. Do what you need to do to prepare TODAY in the best way possible to set yourself up for the future. Get out of these crazy patterns of thinking and, like the Beatles once said in their famous song, "Let it be!" Just allow yourself to be in the moment. The present is not only where the best performances take place, but where the best and most authentic way of living life resides.

Tagline: *BE HERE! Right here, right now!*

STOP JUDGING

Like it or not, people judge all the time. We judge ourselves, we judge others, we compare ourselves to others, and we compare others against others. Athletes, professionals, students and business executives often do this in relation to their performance. Unfortunately, when doing so, they typically fall on the losing side of the judgment spectrum, making it hard to believe in themselves. This constant inner judging simply creates *noise* in one's head. Even more dangerous, people often misinterpret these judgments as a means of pushing and motivating themselves to do well. When you direct your attention toward judgment, you are likely to feel let down every time you fall short of your expectations. Plus, your focus shifts away from where it needs to be in the present to help you succeed. None of that helps push anyone toward a pathway of greatness and success. So many of my athletes get caught up in judgment, and it's one of the first hurdles we need to tackle.

Connor, a college football player I worked with, had loved the game for most of his life. He started playing when he was six years old and had natural talent for the game. Yet, from a very young age, he began judging himself. He was extremely driven and hardworking, but he tended to focus on all the wrong things. His thinking was all about judgment—how well he was playing, how well others were playing, and whether or not he was the best out there on the field on any given day. He judged every game and virtually every play he made on the field. As pressures and expectations grew, so did his judgmental thinking. He started losing his enjoyment and passion for the game, along with his confidence. Once the love of the game was gone, the stress took over. It was hard to sustain motivation, and he started to become anxious and depressed. Then came draft year, and all of these stumbling blocks became too much to handle. Connor's anxiety grew to be so bad that he stopped going to class, was failing out of school and could not return to football. He took a leave of absence and, thankfully, came to me for help.

The nonstop judgment and pressure that had worked for years on the field was no longer working for Connor. After a long and hard road, there is no more football in Connor's life, but he is finally beginning to move in the direction of rebuilding his life. A huge factor in doing so has been learning to let go of self-judgment. Letting go of judgmental thinking unlocks tremendous strain in your mind and frees up space to develop belief and confidence. You don't need to judge. It does not help you to feel good or be good. It only derails your ability to perform at your peak level.

BE YOUR OWN MEASURING STICK

There is no doubt that your thinking and interpretations of performance, events and the world around you shape how you feel and behave. However, it is important to remember that your own thoughts do not exist in isolation of others. You need to be aware not only of the way you think about yourself, but also how you think in relation to those around you.

A common problem I see is constant comparison of self to others. Athletes think, *He's better than me, she's getting more playing time than me, he got drafted and I didn't.* Students think about who got a better mark than they did. Business people think about who got promoted, who is closing more deals or making more money. Parents are busy comparing their families and children to others. Well guess what? Constant comparison is bound to make you feel horrible, and it becomes a huge barrier to building confidence if you allow yourself to continuously go to that place. When people use this comparison approach combined with judgment, they are generally looking in only one direction, and that's up. Even if you are not just looking up, but using comparison to feel good about yourself because you are in a better position than someone else, I still don't like it. Because, guess what? One day you won't be ahead—and then what? All around, comparison is just a bad habit to get into and does not serve you well in the long run.

Have you ever seen athletes on a team who were incredibly

talented when they were little? I'm talking about those players who could wheel through everyone in hockey, football or basketball, or hit homers out of the park in baseball. How many of these young superstars got drafted or continue to play today? On the other hand, how many people do you know who had low marks in school but went on to become highly successful? It happens every day. So, it doesn't really matter where you are in comparison to anyone else. It only matters that you assess where you are and work toward consistent growth and improvement. Being your own measuring stick and building your own progress is what fosters personal development.

A young hockey player named Riley had natural athletic prowess. I started watching him from the time he was nine years old. He was a beast on the ice. He had amazing speed, skill and talent, and when he would wind up to take a shot…watch out! Whipping off shots with the strength and power of a man, Riley often left spectators wowed. Coaches wanted him. Teams wanted him. Year after year, they aggressively recruited him and felt lucky if they landed him. But there was a darker story behind all the glory seen on the ice.

Behind Riley's success, there was a relentless father driving his kid to be the best. Anything less was unacceptable. Riley grew up hearing that message loud and clear. His father's strong, domineering and unrelenting voice drowned out all of the coaches and anyone else who tried to help teach his boy. Riley's father considered the concepts of teamwork and sportsmanship unimportant. For him, the focus was always and only about his kid being superior to others. Whenever someone outplayed Riley, he was continuously beaten down with insults by his father in public. And who knows what happened behind closed doors. The coaches, too, would receive an aggressive earful, which often escalated to threats of violence, if anyone else on the team earned more ice time than Riley. The constant pressure to be better than anyone and everyone else was woven through every aspect of Riley's development and game.

I watched year after year as coaches tried to put up with the father behind the boy. They tolerated this dynamic as long as they could because, I will tell you, Riley had real promise. But eventually, the chaos that came with poor Riley would always become too much, and he would be off to another team within a year or two. Year after year, I watched the fear in Riley's eyes as he would walk out of the dressing room in anticipation of his father's game evaluation.

As time went on, the boy's fear turned into aggression. The aggression was never directed back at his father, but rather, where he felt he could get away with it: at his teammates and in his game. He became the most disliked player in his dressing room, as he constantly blamed others when things didn't go well. He often lost sight of his own game on the ice, as he was busy head-hunting and hitting people just for the sake of knocking them down, often forgetting about making the right play.

Riley continued to be tormented by his father, as did his coaches. He ended up on a top level team, only to be forced to leave the bench in the middle of one game because his father perceived that another player was getting more ice time than his son. I use the word "perceived" because it was not actually the case. At that point, the coaches finally had enough and that was the boy's last day on the team. He moved on and eventually did get drafted in a late round of the OHL draft, despite the fact that he could have been a much higher pick. Eventually however, no longer able to cope both on and off the ice, Riley turned more to trouble than to the game, and he was done. As soon as he was old enough and able to stand up to his father, he quit.

Shattered potential and shattered dreams were the result of a father's drive for his son to be better than everyone else. Constant comparisons made it impossible for the boy to ever live up to expectations. The love of the game through a young boy's eyes turned to dread, fear, and anger; hopes and dreams became a living nightmare.

To a lesser degree, we are all at risk of falling into the comparison trap, be it in the sports world, corporate world, school or everyday life. That's why you must always work to be your own measuring stick. Assess where you are today, notice what needs to be better, and then create an action plan for how to get there. Measure your own progress along the way. Everyone progresses and develops at different rates and stages. The truth is, what everyone else is doing is irrelevant. When you become your own measuring stick, you work to develop personal progress, which builds competence and confidence.

Here's a fun fact for you: Did you know that Albert Einstein could not speak until he was around four years old? At school, all of the other children were talking, but not him. His teachers and parents were so concerned about young Albert. At the end of the day, however, who cares? Of all of those kids, there is only one name we remember today, one name that has been etched in history. No one knows who Albert Einstein's classmates were, but we all know of him. Who cares that everyone could speak before he could? He eventually caught up, and then away he went.

Measuring Stick Exercise: Establish your starting point.

Evaluate honestly where you are at today with respect to the tasks you perform within your field. Do not engage in comparison or judgment. This is simply a self-evaluation.

- **Step 1** – Identify the necessary tasks you need to execute in your performance.
- **Step 2** – Rank yourself on a scale of 1 to10 for each task in

terms of where you believe you are. If you are unsure, then ask your coach, your colleague, or someone you trust to give you an honest opinion.

- **Step 3** – Identify areas that need improvement. Or, choose what you would like to focus your efforts on, and then get to work.

PROACTIVE VERSUS REACTIVE CONFIDENCE

Do you feel confident when things are going well in your life? How about when you evaluate yourself in a positive light? When you have made a great play? Landed a big deal? Earned a good grade? Won a big game? Now ask yourself this: Do you lose confidence when things are not going well? Do you feel bad when you rank low on that task scale above? Or when you have lost a big game, earned a bad grade or screwed up a deal? How about when life is just taking its toll on you? Here is where the problem lies. You are going up, down, and all around, just like a rollercoaster ride. Your confidence is all over the place depending on what's happening to you on any given day. Now, how much control do you think people have when they are riding a rollercoaster? None. You are simply going for a ride. You go where the ride takes you. Think about it. Do you want the same thing happening with respect to your confidence? Absolutely not! You do not want to be reactive with your confidence, constantly reacting to what is happening to you or around you. Living in a re-active state leaves you with absolutely no control. I will say it again. Successful people perform and carry themselves with confidence, irrespective of what is happening to them. In other words, they are exercising proactive confidence.

Let's go back to February 5, 2017 in Houston, Texas. It was Super Bowl LI. The New England Patriots were playing the Atlanta Falcons, with the Falcons dominating the first half of the game.

Tom Brady and the Patriots found themselves down 21 to 0 in the second quarter. They did manage to get on the scoreboard with a field goal just before halftime, ending the first half of the game down 21 to 3. The game was not looking very good for Tom Brady and the Patriots.

One can only imagine what was going through the players' minds and what might have been said in their dressing room during halftime. I will tell you, though, that if they were riding the confidence rollercoaster, allowing themselves to be reactive, they would not have had any fight left to come back with in the second half of the game. So what happened? They did not get caught up in the results. They did not lose their confidence. They continued to work and they continued to believe.

The third quarter of the game did not prove to be much better for the Patriots, as they ended the quarter down 28 to 9. Interestingly enough, no team in Super Bowl history has ever come back from a two touchdown deficit, never mind three touchdowns like the situation the Patriots found themselves in. The fourth quarter however, was all about the Patriots. The score became 28 to 12, then 28 to 20, and with one minute remaining on the clock, the Patriots tied the game at 28 to 28. Another first in Super Bowl history: a tie game. Tom Brady and the New England Patriots went on to win in overtime, 34 to 28, in a legendary game and an epic comeback.

In fact, this comeback was so unimaginable that tennis star Genie Bouchard was gracious enough to make good on a bet she had made after a little Twitter bantering with a 20-year-old University of Missouri student. It all started around the midway point of the game, when Bouchard tweeted, "I knew the Falcons would win, btw." She was then challenged by the 20-year-old student, who tweeted back, "If Patriots win we go on a date?" Bouchard, obviously thinking this one was in the bag, tweeted back, "Sure." And sure enough, not just the game—but the date as well—turned from an inconceivable fantasy to a hard-won reality. Honouring her word, Bouchard flew the student to meet her in New York and took him to a Brooklyn Nets game for their big date out, all on her dime.

I guess Tom Brady and the Patriots, along with student John Gyoehrke, who could now be considered one of the luckiest Patriots fans in history, never stopped believing! It's astounding what can happen when you have the right mindset and carry yourself with confidence. That's where dreams and greatness are born. And "mental toughness," as he said in a postgame interview, is exactly what Tom Brady attributed his team's and his own success to that evening.

PROACTIVE CONFIDENCE

In order to start building your confidence, you need to know what healthy confidence, or proactive confidence, looks like. This is the type of confidence that we want to develop; it is the opposite of reactive confidence. Keep in mind that proactive confidence comes **before** performance. It is built upon **years** of hard work, practice, training, successes and failures. It does **not** come from judging yourself one day at a time, one game at a time, one shift at a time, one grade at a time, or one deal at a time. Healthy confidence recognizes that you will have **both** strengths and weaknesses, good days and bad days. It's about focusing on the **BIG** picture!

Think about this concept in relation to your own life, work, or sport. Which type of confidence have you been functioning with? Proactive or reactive? It is essential to know the definition of healthy confidence in order to begin building the right type of confidence.

HEALTHY SOURCES OF CONFIDENCE

Now that you know what healthy confidence is, you need to

know where to get it from. Healthy confidence comes from healthy sources, such as past success, practice, training and mentorship, preparation, fitness and nutrition, natural talents, and personal strengths and characteristics. As you read on, take note of these different sources that you can draw from. Doing so will help you identify where you can build the type of proactive confidence I am describing. It can also highlight other sources that you may not have in place right now, but may choose to focus on to further develop your confidence.

Past Success

One of the biggest sources of confidence I refer my clients to is past success. Take a few minutes to think about everything you have accomplished within your sport or in your personal or pro-fessional life. Think about when you started and all that you have achieved over your years of hard work, training and experience. Consider what you once couldn't do and now can do. Think about when you messed up or failed and how you overcame the obstacle.

Big Picture Exercise: Focus on your accomplishments over the years.

Reflect upon all of the things you are proud of over the years and write them down in your journal. After you are done, take a look at your list. That's your big picture! Without conscious effort, people forget about all of the things they are proud of and focus instead on what is not going right, or what is breaking their confidence. Remember to have big picture thinking, and stay connected to it.

From time to time, I see people struggle to come up with past successes. If this happens to be you, you may have to dig a little. You may also have to do some self-reflection and ask yourself why you can't seem to identify your accomplishments. What is holding you back from connecting with your strengths? If you are really stuck at ground zero, then let that be where you begin. There is only one way to go from there, and that's up. So, be your own measuring stick and start with small steps. If you are still struggling, then perhaps getting some support by talking to someone could be your step one. You can also ask people who know you well—friends, coaches, family, colleagues, teammates—to reflect with you and let you know what they have seen over the years as your accomplishments. As you begin to take steps forward, you will build your picture.

Practice, Training and Mentorship

Other healthy sources of confidence include your practice, training, coaching, teaching, or mentorship. These are great places to draw confidence from. It is here that you get to try things, fall, fail, learn and keep doing them until you get better. This is also where you have the good fortune to learn from others' knowledge and experience. Make sure you don't miss out on these opportunities, and be mindful of what you are doing, learning and how you are growing. Embrace feedback; don't view it as a threat. Feedback helps you get better, so use it to your advantage.

Preparation/Game Plan

Knowing that you have done the necessary work before you perform is a strong, healthy source of confidence. It is especially important to prepare, and feel prepared, so you can start building your proactive confidence and take it with you into performance. Taking some time to establish pre-game routines and a game plan in your mind is another great way to bolster your confidence. Your mental game plan, along with the hours of hard work and training you put in, will serve to fuel your confidence and allow you to trust in yourself and in your performance. Planning can also alert you if you are not sufficiently prepared so that you can adjust your training and game plan accordingly and get yourself prepared.

> *"By failing to prepare, you are preparing to fail."*
> **– Benjamin Franklin, Founding Father, USA**

Fitness & Nutrition

Let's take a look at fitness and nutrition as good, healthy sources to build confidence, regardless of whether or not you are an athlete. Keeping your body in optimal condition allows you to feel good about yourself both on and off the playing field. And feeling good leads to being good. Beginning to pay attention to what you put into your body, along with exercise and fitness, helps to build a sense of personal competence, which is a great source of proactive confidence.

Natural Talents

As I said earlier, talent is highly overrated. At the same time, however, we are all naturally good at something. So let's briefly take a look at the natural talents you do have. Think about what you are good at. Are you likeable and kind? Do you have size, strength, speed or good game sense? Are you good with people? Are you a natural leader? Are you artistic, scientific or intelligent? Get in touch with some of the natural gifts that you have been blessed with, and make sure to allow yourself to feel good about them. Then work them to your advantage. One of the biggest letdowns is seeing people who are full of wasted potential. Identify your strengths and talents, appreciate them, and then back them up with good positive action.

Personal Qualities & Characteristics

Your own personal qualities and characteristics is a remarkable place to draw confidence from. I love reviewing these with my athletes because this is where I learn about who they really are and who they want to become. Think about your own personal strengths, characteristics and qualities, such as your work ethic, drive, dedication, passion, leadership skills, sacrifices, sportsmanship, being a team player and so on. Doing so will open your eyes to a whole world about yourself that you may have not been paying much attention to. Taking note of your unique qualities will help you see and appreciate yourself in a new and different way.

Confidence Portfolio Exercise: Paint the picture of your unique strengths and capabilities.

Create a portfolio built upon all of the healthy sources of confidence listed above, highlighting the many things you are proud of, have improved upon, have been recognized for and that make you happy. This portfolio can include your own notes, drawings, personal photos, magazine photos, role models, medals, awards, mementos, nutrition plans, letters or comments from others and anything else that resonates for you. Start to build it today and don't ever stop. Day by day, you will see all of the things you have accomplished, including the triumphs and achievements that make you proud and happy. Once you do this, you have your big picture. You will see who you are and what you bring to the game or table. You can look at it anytime you need to draw strength, and doing so will inspire your own sense of proactive confidence.

CONFIDENCE KILLERS

Once you know how and where to draw healthy confidence from, it is important to note the triggers that threaten your confidence. These triggers may come in the form of a person, such as a coach, a parent, a teacher, a colleague, a competitor or a boss. They may also be something that happens, such as making a mistake or failing, getting cut from a team or getting laid off, getting benched or yelled at. Regardless of what it is, just make sure you identify the triggers that put your confidence at risk.

Confidence Killer Exercise: Identify what puts your confidence at risk.

Write down everything that shakes your confidence. Then separate that list into two categories: the things you **can** control and the things you **cannot** control. See the charting examples below.

WHAT KILLS YOUR CONFIDENCE?
e.g. Making Mistakes

CAN CONTROL	CANNOT CONTROL

Once you have completed your list, use the following strategy, target thought and tagline to help you manage your triggers.

Strategy: Take control of what you can, and let go of what you cannot.

Here are some examples of what you can and cannot control:

Can Control	Cannot Control
My reaction to playing time / work environment	Circumstances
My work ethic & effort level	My kids, colleagues' or teammates' mess-ups
My performance	The way others communicate a message
My attitude & response to situations	Other people's thoughts, feelings or reactions
Learning from mistakes & adversity	Refs / colleagues / family members' behaviours
Myself	Mistakes - they have already happened
Letting go of others' expectations & need to please	Someone else's achievement or great play

This exercise likely showed you that much of what you allow to break your confidence is beyond your control. At the end of the day, all you can really control is yourself, your own reactions and behaviours. If you want to be successful, then make sure to bring your confidence with you to the game, office, meeting or classroom. Don't ever let anyone or anything stand in the way of doing that. Believe that you can get there and act accordingly. It may not be to-day. It may not be tomorrow. You may fall along the way, but if you believe in yourself, then you will rise up and keep moving forward.

And eventually, you CAN get there.

"The ones who say they can, and the ones who say they can't, are usually both right."
— **Confucius, Philosopher**

One of the greatest bands of all time shows us how this work is done. Whether you were alive at the time or not, it seems like everyone knows the Beatles–that wild '60s band that turned the music world upside down. But did you know that when the Beatles started out they were rejected by Decca Recording Studios and told they had no future in show business? Do you want to know what one of the key elements to success was for the Beatles? Yes, they were talented, but the Beatles were also extraordinarily proactive with their confidence and their approach to greatness. Success did not come without challenges, rejection and failure along the way. They could not control the timing, they could not control the producers' responses, or the record labels, but they did take control of their own confidence and their belief in themselves and their music. They stayed true to that belief and they went for it. They did what they wanted, when they wanted, how they wanted, and in the way they wanted. They didn't seem to care what anyone else thought.

Here are some quotes from the legendary Beatles before they made it big. I believe it was this pattern of thinking that was a big contributing factor to their success. Take a look at what they had to say in an interview about the start of their journey:

"We wouldn't let 'em put it out. We'd sooner have no contract than put that crap out." —**John Lennon, going against what producers wanted and taking control**

"I suppose we were quite forceful, really, for people in our position. We said we had to live or die with our own song." – **Paul McCartney, reflecting on how they were proactive with their confidence and how they believed in themselves**

"We thought we were the best in Hamburg and Liverpool—it was just a matter of time before everybody else caught on." –**John Lennon**

"We were the best f#$%'ing group in the…world… and believing that is what made us what we were." –**John Lennon**

Power Statement Exercise: Develop your personal power statements.

Create 3 to 5 personal power statements that you will use daily to speak to yourself in a confident way. Choose a time of day, such as when you wake up in the morning or before you leave the house, when you will say them out loud.

Here are a few examples:

1. I am a strong and capable individual who is eager to learn and grow.
2. I will give 100% effort as I work toward my goals, no matter what is happening.
3. I do not give up or give in when things go wrong. I use challenge to learn and drive harder.
4. I know what I want and I will not be denied.
5. I can do this! I've got this!

CHAPTER 4

MANAGING EXPECTATIONS

THE PRESSURE ILLUSION

Belief in yourself helps breed success, but as we see, there are also many triggers that kill confidence and impede progress toward success. One of the more subtle, silent killers that robs people of their confidence and merits special attention is expectations. These are the demands that we place on ourselves. They are the *shoulds* and the *musts* that we feel we have to live up to in order to achieve. They are also the real or self-imposed demands we take on from others, such as coaches, colleagues, parents, teachers, and teammates. Too often, we mistake these expectations as a push toward success, when in reality, they end up causing more harm than good.

I once worked with a quiet, shy, intelligent and extremely skilled tennis player named Kaitlyn. This girl's work ethic was off the charts. She consistently worked and trained. Outside of school, tennis was all she knew. After spending countless hours on the court over the years, she developed into quite the player. Kaitlyn gained a great deal of recognition for her game. From the time she was in tenth grade, she was heavily sought after by top U.S. colleges, including Ivy League schools. As time moved on and she got closer to college, her expectations for herself became stronger, as did everyone else's, and her game deteriorated. The problem? Kaitlyn expected herself to be perfect. Every shot had to be right on. Every point had to be hers to win. Her thought process was focused on how hard she worked and the fact that she outworked every other tennis player she knew. As such, Kaitlyn drew conclusions around the need and expectation for perfection. She also believed this sense of perfection was what she needed to show the tennis world. Whenever she fell short of her strict expectations, she became frustrated, and her confidence was shaken. She started to unravel right there on the court. She became rattled, emotional and uncomposed while she was playing.

Concern set in among the scouts who had traveled to watch her play, which made Kaitlyn even more distressed. She started losing matches against people she had easily beaten in the past. The scouts and schools that had been excited about her for years were slowly losing interest. The phone calls and visits started to dwindle, which chipped away at Kaitlyn's confidence until there was nothing left. Kaitlyn became depressed and anxious, and fearful of losing her opportunity at an NCAA scholarship. That's when she ended up in my office.

Kaitlyn and I worked together to flush out all of the underlying expectations and pressures she was holding on to, along with the demands she was carrying into competition. This noise clouds your mind, causing you to continuously judge yourself while you are competing or performing, and as we have already learned, judgment is not helpful to performance. If you are so busy judging yourself in game, or in life in general, how are you supposed to concentrate on your task at hand and what you are trying to accomplish?

Focusing on pressure and expectations prior to performance only drives nerves and anxiety in anticipation of how things will go. The constant underlying fear of messing up will be ever present. Then, all of this noise and anxiety gets dragged into your performance. How do you think that plays out? What goes through your head if you believe you *shouldn't* mess up and then you do? When it happens, as it eventually will, that becomes the moment your negative and self-critical thinking kicks in. You may try to shake it off, but it's still there, kind of lingering. And what is bound to happen next? You mess up again! And that noise and negative thinking gets stronger and stronger until, as in Kaitlyn's case, it chips away at your confidence.

How are you supposed to be great when you believe you are falling short of what you think you *should* be doing, and consistently losing your confidence? It's just not possible. Your mind is focused on all of this noise, which moves you away from the task at hand—competing, performing or doing what you need to do. You have gone from being anxious beforehand, to judging yourself during, to feeling bad both during and afterwards, and so the vicious cycle begins.

EXPECTATIONS: REASONABLE OR RIDICULOUS?

So, what are your expectations? What are the underlying demands that you place upon yourself? What are the expectations you have for your children, your colleagues, or those you lead, coach or teach?

Here is a list of some of the most common ones that I hear from athletes and clients. Can you relate to any of them?

ATHLETES	PERSONAL & HIGH-LEVEL PERFORMERS	PARENTS OF ATHLETES & LEADERS/COACHES
Need to win	Be successful	Want them to do well
Put up points	Get noticed	Be successful
Be successful	Need to impress	Want them to be happy
Get noticed	Close this deal	Want them to develop skills
Shouldn't mess up	No room for error	Be respectful
Make perfect passes	Be great	Be a good teammate
Can't be a minus	Be better than...	Work hard
Don't disappoint teammates	Stand out	Try their best
Can't let down parents	Make money	Follow rules & systems
Impress scouts/coach	Project has to be successful	Build character
Don't mess up or get yelled at	Get a bonus	Give back to the game
Should be more focused	Numbers have to be good	Develop good people
Shouldn't be nervous	Take this guy down	Produce
Need a good warm up	Get this client	Win games/deals
Should be more confident	Lose weight	Don't let me down
Need to make this team/ next level	Be healthy	Instill a love of the game or passion for the work

FOR ATHLETES & HIGH-LEVEL PERFORMERS

For people who need to be focused on performance, these expectations simply generate unneeded pressure. They detract from a present and process-oriented focus relating to task execution, which is what will lead to the success you are looking for. Expectations simply drive judgment that will ultimately get inside your head and inhibit your ability to focus effectively. You do not want to bring your expectations into performance with you. They will set you on that confidence rollercoaster, putting you at risk every time things do not play out the way you wish.

FOR PARENTS, COACHES & LEADERS

The expectations that parents, coaches and leaders tend to bring forth to their children, athletes, students or employees, generally come with good underlying intentions, such as: *I want you to develop, be successful, try hard, etc.* The question is, do their actions and interactions with those they impact genuinely match their words and desires? When you yell at kids for a mistake, do you think that allows them to have fun? When you give the post-game analysis in the car ride home, do you think your child hears you and takes in what you are saying? When you say that all you care about is effort and that you wouldn't be angry if only your child had tried, do you really think they didn't try or don't want to do well? Or do you think it is possible that maybe the child doesn't have the right coping skills in place to know how to handle a difficult situation? Not every kid knows how to deal effectively with mistakes, frustrations, losing, or not playing well.

Similarly, if you are leading a team of people in the sports world or corporate world, do you lead by example and equip your team with the necessary skills and tools to be successful? Or do you just demand and drive them with expectations?

Of course, you want all the right things—drive, self-confidence, good results, success—but are you giving yourself, your children, your athletes, your students, or your team, the right skills to be able to create those things? It doesn't help to tell someone to be happy or successful when they are struggling and they don't know how to get there.

FOR EVERYONE

I have given you a lot to think about and asked a lot of questions. Now for the big question: Are your thoughts and expectations reasonable and rational, or are they completely unattainable? Find me a player on your team, or in your sport, who has never messed up. Find me an athlete who plays a perfect game all of the time. Find me someone who never makes a mistake, in sport, in school, in business or in life. You can't. It's not possible!

What you are asking from yourself is often unreasonable and unattainable and yet, you become focused on it and driven by these expectations. You judge yourself moment by moment, and then feel awful when you fall short. I know you may think expectations motivate you, but that is an error in your thinking. The only time expectations work well for you is if everything is falling into place exactly as you planned. But tell me, how often does that happen on the playing field, in the corporate world, raising children and a family, or in life for that matter? It doesn't! If you hold yourself to these ideal standards, you will no doubt end up falling short. It might be today, it might be tomorrow, but I promise you, it will happen. Sport and life are unpredictable, so it's time to let go of all expectations. I know you want to fulfill those expectations that you set. I get it! But driving yourself with expectations does not help you. It hurts you. So, let me show you a better way.

"The Great One" Wayne Gretzky, true to the name and arguably one of the best hockey players in history, lit up the ice in his 1979 to 1980 rookie season in the NHL. Not only did he live up to all expectations, but he also seemed to exceed them. He tied Marcel Dionne as the leading point scorer in the league, became the youngest player to score 50 goals in a season, and won the Hart Trophy being named NHL's most valuable player. Not too bad for a first year in the big leagues. The greatness didn't end there, as he went on to set new records the following year. Gretzky seemed unstoppable.

Fast forward a little. It was the Canada Cup in 1981, when six of the top hockey nations were set to compete in an international tournament. The pressure was on, as expectations for Gretzky and Team Canada mounted. Gretzky, the natural goal scorer, was surprisingly held off the score sheet in Canada's game against Czechoslovakia. It was a highly unusual experience for The Great One. He bounced back, however, in the round robin games and the semi-final game, defeating the U.S. to set the stage for the highly anticipated Canada vs. Soviet Union final. There was hype, clash, anticipation and excitement. The first half of the game was everything everyone had hoped for with the score tied at 1 to 1. You could say that Canada was dominating the game to that point, but the Soviet goaltender Vladislav Tertiak stood on his head denying Canada the lead. That's where the excitement ended—for Canada and Wayne Gretzky at least. The Soviets took control of the game, demolishing the great Gretzky and Team Canada with an 8 to 1 victory. Gretzky took the loss hard, saying, "I played so badly, they should have sent me to Siberia." He also said, "I let my country down." Now that's a heavy load to bear.

Following the loss, Gretzky took some time off to recover and think about what happened. Upon reflection, he was able to analyze his style of play and identify what he felt was not working. He then focused on how to change it. Instead of staying tied up with expectations, he figured out how to reinvent himself on the ice. Despite the fact that Gretzky had already achieved success like no other in his first two NHL seasons, he came back to his next season in 1981 to 1982 with his new approach to the game. You won't believe what happened next. Not quite at the halfway point of the season, Gretzky shattered the record book as everyone once knew it. On December 30, 1981, he scored his 50th goal of the season, at only 39 games in. Among his multitudes of records set, this could be considered to stand out as one of the greatest.

Gretzky faced his adversity and used it to come back stronger. I am sure it wasn't easy for him at the time, as failure is never easy. But look at what he did when he was challenged. If The Great One had to take some time to rebuild and figure things out, then why can't you do the same in your life? In fact, it is essential to use challenge, time and self-reflection to your advantage. It is amazing what can happen when you shift your focus from overloaded pressure and expectations toward executing the tasks that will produce the desired outcome. Success does not come from telling yourself you need to win or do well, or that you can't make a mistake. Success comes from figuring out the how-to in terms of making it happen.

Target Thought: *Failure is simply a chance to try again a little better the next time.*

FOCUS ON THE PROCESS

It is now time to go from the demands of what you want to the actual execution and steps you need to take to get there. As an athlete or high-level performer, you've got to learn to let go of your expectations and transfer that energy to a **focus on the process**. Ask yourself what it takes to be successful. Identify the specific tasks you need to execute in order to create the success you are looking to achieve. That's where you need to direct your attention. You could be one of the most engaged, hardest working, and focused people in the world, but if you are not focused on the process of what it is you are doing, then you are NOT concentrating on the right things. Why do you think you can perform certain skills in practice or training, but not in games or high performance situations? No one has stolen your ability, your skill level, or your athletic prowess. It's your mental game that is not intact. You need to refocus yourself on execution and fall in love with the process. When your mind is paying attention to the right things, you are more likely to do the right things, and the results will start to take care of themselves.

The best athletes and performers get into what is referred to as *the zone*—the place where people perform at their best. That zone comes when you are completely engaged in what you are doing and are focused in that very moment on the process. It comes when you let go of all the noise, worries, expectations, pressures and results. This is when you are locked in and giving 100% to what needs to be done. We give power to what we focus on, so if you are devoting 10% of your focus to how good your opponent or the other team is, 20% to worrying about how you will do, 10% to what the coach or clients are thinking, 10% to needing to impress the scouts, clients, the boss, or your colleagues, 10% to worrying about letting people down and so on and so on, then what are you left with in terms of focusing on your game or task at hand? Not nearly enough.

The first step is to become aware of all that noise in order to flush it out. I sit with my athletes and together we extract all of the underlying thoughts, pressures and expectations they take into performance with them. We categorize these stressors into four different sections:

1. **Result-related:** Anything that is focused directly on results
   Example: I need to win, score, put up points, hit financial targets or sales, and so on.

Note: I recognize that you may need to hit these targets in the reality of what you do, but there is a difference between setting these as overall goals versus carrying them into performance on a day-to-day basis.

2. **The quality of your own performance:** What you demand and expect from yourself
   Example: I should be one of the best. I need to play a perfect game.

3. **Other oriented:** What others expect of you, whether spoken or unspoken, as well as what you expect of others
   Example: My coach shouldn't yell. I can't let down my parents/teammates.

4. **Mental game related:** Any of the mental demands you place on yourself
   Example: I should be more focused, more confident, I need a good warm up, etc.

Together, my clients and I work to come up with a comprehensive list of all of their expectations and put them down on paper. Then, we have some fun as we reverse roles and I read their expectations aloud. I pretend I am the athlete, I have a big game coming up and I am feeling very anxious. It's impactful what these expectations sound like when you hear them all together. I notice myself getting worked up as I fire them off, one after the other. Of course, I do play it up a little, but wow, what pressure people put themselves under! The funniest part is after all that, we come to the mental-related expectations at the bottom of the list where I find things like, *I shouldn't be nervous*, or *I should be more confident and relaxed*. I peer over at my client with a sly look and ask, "Now, how on earth are you supposed to do that with all of this going on in your head?" That's the *AHA!* moment when people finally hear what they have been doing to themselves. They look up at me with big eyes and a sheepish smile and I know I've got them. They recognize the barriers they have erected and the chains they have been performing with, and I know we are ready to start making some progress.

I once worked with a Minor Midget hockey goaltender named Jack who moved to Toronto from the U.S. for his OHL draft year. As any 15-year-old boy moving away from home for the first time to play hockey would agree, this was a significant life change. Jack came to Canada with some nerves, but mostly with a lot of excitement and anticipation for the biggest year to come in minor hockey. There were, of course, some challenges as well as a lot of things to get used to, like a new school, a new team, new people, new friends, a new billet family and so on, but Jack was ready to take it all on. All for the love of the game. It is remarkable to see just how much these kids will sacrifice to follow their dreams—until the day the dream and the boy start to get broken.

It wasn't long before Jack's hockey experience started to deteriorate. His coach became increasingly abusive, both verbally and emotionally. Early on, there were warning signs for Jack and his family but they pushed them aside. Far too often, the drive and commitment to the game, and everything one sacrifices for it, puts blinders on people's eyes and overrides their instincts. Jack kept working however, despite the fact that his coach would consistently verbally and emotionally abuse him, telling him how horrible he was. The coach would pull Jack out of the game with the first goal he let in. He would yo-yo him back and forth in and out of a single game so many times that it was hard to keep track. He would address the team between periods, telling them that their goalie was *sh*t* so they had better score a goal because Jack had no idea how to stop a puck. He had some other things to say to Jack as well, but the language is not appropriate for this book, so I will leave it to your imagination.

Remember, this is a 15-year-old boy, living in a new country alone, with no family, trying to make new friends. Not so easy to do when your coach is constantly humiliating you in front of your teammates and blaming you for the team's losses and misfortunes. A once confident and excited Jack became anxious, scared and angry. What was going to happen to his hockey career? What was going to happen to his chances of getting drafted, which he had sacrificed everything for? Understandably, his game play and his confidence started to suffer. When he did get the chance to play, he was so fearful of making a mistake that he played safe and scared. Yet, he was determined to prove his coach wrong. He was trying. He was hanging in there, but his game play became inconsistent. He could make a great save one minute and then let in the softest goal the next. He was all over the place. Of course, his coach and his environment were the trigger for the problems, but that wasn't going to change. What needed to change was how Jack was interpreting and reacting to the events going on around him.

Jack had become driven by thoughts and expectations which had been formed as a result of his situation. He strongly believed some of the following unproductive thoughts/expectations:

- I need to play perfectly.
- There is no room for error.
- I need to prove my coach wrong.
- I need to get more playing time.
- I can't do anything to provoke my coach.

Talk about playing under the gun. It is no wonder why Jack's performance started to unravel.

Jack and I worked together to help him deal with all of the emotions he felt in relation to his coach. This introspection helped him to cope. It helped him handle the fact that the coach sat him on the bench for the final eight games of the season and most of the playoffs as well. During that time, Jack learned to work on his mental game. He used it as an opportunity to become a more mentally tough hockey player. He employed a new approach, a new mindset, and his experience felt more tolerable. It didn't change the fact that the situation sucked, but during that time, Jack finally came to understand how his expectations were killing his game and his mood as well. As I always work to find the bright side of things, even in a dark situation, I told Jack how lucky we were to have all of this time to break down his game and focus him on the process. I joked around with him and told him that we owe it all to his coach for not playing him, and for giving us all of this extra time to work, think, and practice the new mental skills he had learned. We managed to laugh about it.

The reality was, he wasn't playing, which provided us with the luxury of time to develop a process-oriented approach. While this was happening, Jack's team qualified to play in the OHL Cup following the season, which is one of the most prominent and exciting minor hockey tournaments in the world, played by many of the greats we know today like Connor McDavid, P.K. Subban, Taylor Hall, Drew Doughty and Jonathan Tavares.

Even though Jack was handling the situation so much better, he was still a little down about the whole OHL Cup situation, and I understood. It was to be a highlight moment in his hockey career, but he no longer expected to get a chance to play. Nevertheless, Jack had worked hard on his mental game and definitely used this experience as an opportunity to become a more well-rounded athlete, both mentally and physically.

And then, much to his surprise, Jack miraculously got the start for game two of the OHL Cup, as the other goaltender had played quite poorly in the first game. For the first time that season, he was able to step out onto the ice and let go of his expectations. He knew exactly what he wanted to focus on and that was his game, his positioning, his tracking of the puck and the players—the process. And that's what he did. There was no judgment, just 100% focus and effort directed toward what he could control. Nothing else mattered, not even the coach. Jack played the game one shot at a time, with a clear mind, and no noise in his head. Not only did his team go on to win that game, but Jack was awarded MVP (Most Valuable Player) from all of the players on the ice. This was a pretty impressive turn of events. As I said, when you focus on the "right" things necessary to create success, that is, the execution, the results take care of themselves.

If you want to win games, then you may need to focus on teamwork, following systems and staying positive. If you want to score goals or put up points, then you have to drive hard to the net, look for an opening, and take shots. If you want to be happy, then you have to stop focusing on negative thoughts and engaging in situations that rob you of happiness, or allowing others to do so, and use that energy to do things that make you happy. If you want to succeed in the boardroom, then you have to do your research, prepare your strategy and engage in effective communication techniques. If you want to build a successful business then you need to know everything there is to know about your product or service, know your target market and do the research on your competitors. These are just some examples that can help to refocus you on the process of whatever it is you are doing.

I use the word W.I.N. with my clients to help them remember to always come back to this acronym. If you want a winning attitude and a winning game or performance, then use the tagline below and keep asking yourself the following question: *What's Important Now?*

Target Thought: *Expectations are more hurtful than helpful.*

Tagline: *W. I. N. - What's Important Now?*

When you answer that question, no matter what situation you are in, you will be able to identify the things you need to work at doing. If you are down in a game, then maybe you need to focus on offensive play. If you have made a mistake, then you need to figure out how to fix it. If you have a big competition, performance, meeting, or presentation coming up, then make sure you prepare appropriately.

Expectations Exercise: Flush out your expectations and build a better approach using the step-by-step guide and the chart example below.

1. Write down all of the expectations and underlying thinking you may be carrying into your life, your work, or your sport right now.
2. Go through the four categories of expectations discussed earlier, and think about what your demands are in each of those areas.
3. Read them aloud and allow yourself to hear the added pressure you have put yourself under.
4. Get ready to let these expectations go, and as you do, put a nice big X through each one.
5. For each of the expectations, answer the following questions: Is this reasonable and realistic? Is this productive for me?
6. Use this Refocus Statement technique: Replace each expectation with a more productive or realistic statement that is manageable and that you have control over.
7. Then, in the column beside your Refocus Statement, put bullet points for each task you will execute to help you achieve success in that area. We call these Process Goals.

EXPECTATIONS	REFOCUS STATEMENTS	PROCESS GOALS
Athlete Example: Must win	The reality is that everyone wants to win, including my opponent. My job is to give 100% effort from start to finish, no matter what is happening.	• Use speed • Be aggressive • Take shots • Let go of mistakes • Stay in the present

You can use the example above and adapt it to your situation in the corporate world, in your business, classroom, dressing room or your life in general. This homework applies to coaches, parents, teachers, and corporate leaders as well. Don't just do the exercise in relation to yourself, but also in relation to those you work with and those you lead.

If you are driving people with expectations such as, *We have to win, I just want you to do well,* or even *I want you to be happy,* it's time to stop. Even if you are not overtly saying these exact words but they are being expressed by your behaviour, tone, and body language, you need to become aware of the messages you are communicating and then change those that are not productive. Such expectations can only disadvantage the people you lead, the children you raise, or those you work with. Instead, help them figure out the right things to focus on to improve performance. Praise effort, not results, as it is that consistent effort that will eventually lead them to success.

RELIEVING THE PRESSURE

It's time to put down what I refer to in my practice as the *pres-*

sure gun. Stop living, competing and performing with a virtual gun to your head, under so much pressure, thinking *I have to do this* or *I can't do that.* When you do that, all your body hears is *uh-oh,* and a certain part of your brain called the amygdala is triggered. The amygdala is like an alarm or warning signal that alerts us so we can deal with potentially dangerous situations. In an emergency situation, it is there to prepare our body to either mobilize itself into action, or to escape—otherwise known as the fight or flight response. Its purpose is to help us to survive. The problem, however, is your body can't tell the difference between real danger and perceived danger. As soon as the brain receives the *uh-oh* message, its alarm is sounded, triggering a surge of adrenalin released throughout the body.

To help my clients better understand this phenomenon and how it relates to their performance, I ask them to tell me how they would feel if they were held at gunpoint. The most common response is obviously nervous and scared. I then ask them to describe what scared feels like in their bodies. Here are some of the responses I receive:

- racing heart
- shaky
- muscle tension
- butterflies/sick feeling in stomach
- racing thoughts
- difficulty concentrating
- dry mouth
- difficulty making decisions
- frozen; can't move

I go on to ask clients whether they experience these same feelings when they are nervous about an upcoming game, business meeting, presentation, or test, and most reply yes. That's because they have sounded the alarm and their body is doing what it's supposed to be doing—responding to a danger signal. It's just like when you set the alarm on your phone and you set the volume level at which it will sound. We do the same thing in our brains. The stronger the signal, the louder the alarm will sound, resulting in increased severity of the symptoms and bodily response. Because your body doesn't know if you are in real or perceived danger, your bodily response may not be proportionate to the situation.

If your expectations are that you have to do well, that you have to win, and that you can't mess up, doesn't it make sense that you are nervous? The fact is you will never be the best athlete, student, professional, or anything else for that matter, if you are too nervous and scared while performing or competing because you are essentially performing with that gun to your head. You are under too much pressure!

You will often hear sport psychologists say that pressure is just an illusion. It's kind of true. However, I have been around athletes, sports, and high-level performers such as surgeons long enough to know that there are pressures at every age and stage. They are real for you, I get that. Game seven of the playoffs is do or die. That's real. Athletic scholarships are on the line, that's real. Million-dollar deals, that's real. Having someone's life in the palm of your hand, that's *real*. But go with me on this for a moment. It's still the same game, or boardroom, or operating room. You play by the same rules, in the same equipment, and you know how to do what you do. You have played the game hundreds and thousands of times before. That doesn't change. The only thing that changes is the way you think about what you are doing. It is the thinking that creates the pressure, the nerves and the anxiety. A doctor in the operating room with a body cut open and bleeding everywhere literally has someone's life in their hands. Is this real pressure? Yes. But that doctor cannot allow their focus to linger on catastrophic worry such as *OMG, this person could die now.* They must be focused on what they know and on what they need to do to try and save the patient's life.

It is also important to note that some sense of pressure and adrenalin is good and helpful. It can motivate you, drive you and get your body prepared to go into battle. It does make sense to feel some nerves before a big game, big deal, new situation, big exam or big presentation. Being nervous is normal, and usually those feelings subside once you get focused on the task at hand. If, however, your danger signal is too strong and the nerves take over, then it's impossible to perform your best. The problem occurs when the pressure becomes too much or when the interpretation of it is too much and you move into that danger zone. Here, the ringtone on that alarm is set too high, and the pressure shifts from helping you with your performance to hurting you.

So, pay attention to those underlying thoughts and expectations triggering your alarm system and put the gun down! The puck, the ball, or the end result doesn't know it's do or die. Only you do. So, learn to fall in love with the process and keep working to shift your focus in that direction. Check out how Lebron James does it.

> *"There is a lot of pressure put on me, but I don't put a lot of pressure on myself. I feel if I play my game it will take care of itself."*
> – **Lebron James, Basketball Star**

Target Thought: *The right amount of pressure creates diamonds. Too much pressure crumbles to dust.*

This cute ten-year-old boy named Johnny walked into my office one day with his dad, who was a high-level golfer. Johnny was a young athlete who played competitive golf and hockey. There were definitely some hopes and expectations from his father for Johnny to advance competitively in golf. The problem was that Johnny hated golf. Or did he? He hated losing, and he hated when his friends would outshoot him. He hated when he blew a shot, and he hated any moment when things did not go exactly as he wanted. No wonder he hated golf!

Johnny shared some of the same frustrations when he played hockey, but these feelings were not quite as intense, as he managed through his interpretation of the situation to share the sense of responsibility with the team. Doing so lessened his personalized sense of failure. His issue with hockey, however, was that he so badly wanted to be a goalie. His eyes lit up when he spoke about being in net, but he wouldn't dare tell anyone that he loved and even dreamed about goaltending. With a devilish look in his eye, he explained that the only reason he shared this information with me was that he knew I couldn't tell anyone. (I had just finished giving him and his dad my little chat about confidentially before his dad left the room.) Johnny proceeded to tell me there was no point in talking about his dream anyway, because he would never go for it. Going for it would mean he would have to start from scratch, which meant he wouldn't be very good at it. "So, it will never ever happen," he concluded. This little guy was unhappy, unmotivated, and completely stressed out. He hated going golfing, he was hiding a secret about hockey, and he certainly did not want to be sitting in my office.

I had to work hard to win Johnny over. We played games, we joked around, we watched videos, and finally, I managed to engage him. Then our work began. We worked intensely on understanding pressure and expectations, and we had the opportunity to flush them all out. We then worked to replace each and every one of them. First came our refocus statements with our new, more reasonable, realistic and productive thoughts to replace the old ones. Then, we built his process goals. After some time, Johnny began to get it and there was a palpable sense of relief. It was like this dark cloud was lifted off of him and that became a turning point in our work together. I watched as Johnny began to change. He understood where his nerves, anxiety and unhappiness were coming from. He learned to put down the pressure gun he was unproductively motivating himself with every day. He learned how to approach his sports differently. Through the process, he found his voice and his courage.

You can now find Johnny on the golf course having fun and playing with his friends, but he no longer golfs competitively. Better yet, you can see his smile light up through his new goalie mask. Once he learned to let go of the fears and pressure he was carrying around, he gained tremendous motivation, along with a willingness to start from scratch to become a goalie. He worked hard with a goalie coach. He was finally engaged. He did all of the right things with his training. And instead of starting in house league, Johnny had the courage to go to rep tryouts. He didn't make the higher level team he had hoped for, but he did make the next rep team a level down. For the first time in a long time, Johnny felt proud of his accomplishments. He is now happy to be involved in sport and has learned to love playing, all without unnecessary pressure.

CHAPTER 5

FEAR OF FAILURE

LEARNING TO FAIL FORWARD

I'll never forget the life-changing day that I reinvented my career. No major event happened; no one was born, no one died. It was the day, however, that I decided to face my fears and move forward in spite of them. I had been working for many years in a general counselling practice when I got an opportunity to do some mental game workshops with a group of young players in a hockey camp. The founder and head instructor of the hockey school believed you could not develop an elite athlete without addressing the psychological side of the game. His idea of delivering mental game workshops for players sounded interesting to me. I liked the progressive thinking, so I agreed to sign on. I did some research and put together the workshops. The response was overwhelmingly positive. People were intrigued. Parents started approaching me and I gained a number of individual clients as a result.

As time went on, I began working with athletes in my practice and I was loving it. The hockey instructor started pushing me to do more and more performance coaching. He encouraged me to leave my safe little psychotherapy practice and specialize in the area of sport and performance psychology on a full-time basis. He kept telling me there was a need in the market, that it was a whole untapped area. Exciting? Yes. But untapped also meant unknown.

I was afraid. What if it failed? Was it worth it to start all over again to follow this newfound passion? I had spent 15 years running my practice. It was safe and comfortable. I knew what to expect. I made a decent living. What was wrong with that? Nothing really. Still, for some reason, I couldn't get this new idea out of my head.

I carried on running my psychotherapy practice for a while, and enjoyed bringing in new athletes to work with. At the same time, I continued doing sport psychology workshops at the hockey camps. I also had another insider perspective at the time when it came to competitive sports—through my personal experience with my own children. My sons were trying out all different sports, from hockey to soccer to baseball, and soon, we settled into being a hockey family. And boy let me tell you, when it came to youth sports, I saw some crazy things. I witnessed pretty intense emotions, I saw kids getting yelled at when they made mistakes, coaches screaming and swearing at kids, kids being sat on the sidelines or the bench, kids falling apart when they failed or the training got tough, coaches being paid off to get kids on teams, kids being given money for private school education to recruit them to teams, parents getting into fights, pressures, demands, expectations, and a whole lot of drama.

All of this intensity got me thinking. A lot. It seemed to me that we are treating kids like miniature adults in the world of competitive youth sports. There was just so much stuff going on that I began to wonder how I could help my own kids deal with all of the stressors and still enjoy the journey. How could I help them be great despite all the craziness? How would I help myself be great for them and for the other people I work with? How would I help others to find greatness within themselves? These burning questions consumed me. I continued to study, take more courses, and learn every day. Working with athletes and in the area of sport was a passion. But at the end of the day, would I really leave my practice to build a whole new one?

Soon afterward, a brand new rink and state of the art facility was about to be built in Toronto. It was going to be a beautiful new hockey hub in Downsview Park. Even the GTHL, the largest minor hockey association in the world, was going to move there. I knew this was my chance. I had done the research, I had done the work, and I had gained some great experience. If I was ever going to make a move, this was the place that I would want to be. So why wasn't I jumping all over it? I realized that it was a risk and I didn't want to fail. At the same time, however, I knew that I could never grow if I gave into that fear. I had done the preparation and work with my athletes was going very well. It was time to just go for it. Finally, with some thought, planning, and self-reflection, it was decision day. It was not without fear, but I made the choice to believe in myself and do it anyway.

In my psychotherapy practice, I was already a specialist in working with people's thinking, feelings and behaviours, so I went on to apply my knowledge to sport and performance. I worked count-less hours at my computer doing research, reading books, taking courses, earning certifications and learning. I rented an office in the newly built rink, and I did it. At first, I had very few clients and I often sat alone in an empty office. There were days that I felt like I didn't know what I was doing. So, what did I do? I learned more about running a business, and more about sport and performance psychology. I learned from every mistake I made, and I kept at it until I figured it out. But all along, I never stopped believing that I *could* figure it out, even if I didn't have all the answers.

Then, somehow, my efforts began to pay off. My clients were pleased and spreading the word. My practice started growing and growing and growing. I started meeting amazing people. I got hired to work with teams and organizations. I found myself in meetings with the coaching staff of the Pittsburgh Penguins, management at the Toronto Maple Leafs and player development guys at the Toronto Blue Jays. I was being interviewed by reporters on TV and for print. I expanded my company by opening a new division. I became the first Mental Performance Coach in the OHL to join a team's staff and season with the Peterborough Petes. Then, I began writing this book. Today, I am so grateful to be where I am. Some days, I almost can't believe it myself. But getting here was not without fear. Was I afraid that venturing into new territory could be a mistake? Absolutely. And I did it anyway! I always tell my clients that the unwillingness to face fear of failure and the choice to stay safe may keep them comfortable, but nothing great ever grows there.

Tagline: *Greatness comes outside of comfort zones.*

Through this experience, I had to look my fear square in the eye on many occasions and decide what I was going to do about it. The truth is that when I failed at something, it was never really quite as bad as I feared it would be. I simply figured out how to deal with it, picked myself up, and carried on. I continuously used my W.I.N. statement and asked myself: *What's important now?* Answering that question allowed me to re-adjust when necessary. Whether things were going well or falling apart, I asked and I answered. From there, I focused on the things I needed to do under those circumstances to be successful.

How do you view failure? If you fear it or think it's bad, then change that thinking! Failure might not feel great, but in actuality, it is part of life and essential for growth. When you change the thoughts about failure, your fear will decrease, at least enough so that you can move forward in spite of it. Then gaining the right skills and executing the necessary tasks related to the desired outcome or situation keeps you moving forward. Taking these steps definitely helped me, even if that meant going back to the drawing board at times and starting over again. Without doing that, I would never be where I am today.

Target Thought: *Failure is an essential part of building success - not the opposite of it.*

Please remember, you are human and you will fail. I don't mean to be the bearer of bad news, but we could all use a reminder. The road to success is not a smooth one. You WILL mess up. You WILL make mistakes, and you WILL fail along the way. Failure is inevitable, so I don't know why it has become such a dirty word in our society. People hate to fail! They fear it and want to avoid it at all costs. They don't realize that failure can be one of the greatest motivators and learning opportunities, if used in the right way. It is a tremendous catalyst for growth.

Young, talented athletes, good enough to be high-round draft picks who make their team in their rookie year, often find that first year to be a tough one. I have seen it over and over again. Playing time is hard to come by, and sitting on the bench, or even being stuck in the stands as a healthy scratch is not uncommon. The truth is, many of these athletes simply don't know how to handle the adversity of not getting played. All they want to do is play, and that's not happening. They feel like they have failed. Again, it comes back to those expectations. If these guys could just hang in there and go with the process of what it means to be a rookie and earn their stripes, they would get to where they want to be, and enjoy the experience a whole lot more. The fact is, mistakes, and even failure, simply provide us with the opportunity to try again a little better the next time. If people can keep moving forward and work to get better regardless of the circumstances, then eventually, that is exactly what will happen.

WHY PEOPLE GIVE UP

There is an old Chinese proverb that I just love. It goes like this: *The temptation to quit is usually the strongest just before you are about to succeed.* That's because if you believe that failure is bad, then you're likely to stop trying, make excuses, or give up, when you come face to face with it. Of course, there's no telling how far you could have gotten, if only you could have hung in a little, or even a lot, longer. The worst part is that by giving up your belief in your ability to keep going, you end up defeating yourself. Here are some of the most common reasons people give up:

- It's too hard
- They got hurt (physically and/or mentally)
- They messed up/made mistakes
- Failure
- Lack of confidence
- Someone said they couldn't do it
- They felt they lacked skill
- Rejection
- Didn't get drafted
- Didn't make a team/got cut from a team
- Didn't get a job/promotion
- Business/financial struggles
- Results not coming quick enough
- Comparison to others
- Someone spoke badly of them
- Situational
- It's easier to quit
- Life struggles

A young gymnast came to see me one day because she could

no longer do a floor sequence. It was a roundoff, back handspring, back tuck. Chloe had performed these moves a million times before, but she simply couldn't do it anymore. She told me it was like her brain felt stuck and wouldn't allow her body to move. I delved a little deeper and found out that a few months back, Chloe had taken a bad fall while she was doing that sequence. The fall hurt her both physically and mentally. Her back was in some pain, and she felt humiliated and embarrassed. *AHA, there it was,* I thought. *That was the turning point where things went south.* When I mentioned my theory to her however, she wasn't buying it. Chloe told me I didn't really understand her. She explained that she knew that particular incident wasn't the problem because she had managed to do the sequence several times after the fall. She told me there was just something wrong with her and her brain.

Through our work together, I helped Chloe to see the situation in a new way. The fall was the trigger that set everything into motion. It had triggered a whole set of thinking patterns and beliefs around the sequence, particularly the back tuck, the point at which she had fallen. There was a lot of thinking going on, but the underlying root was, *I am afraid to fail and fall again.* Even though the initial fall hurt physically, the only real injury was an emotional one. Quite simply, Chloe didn't want that fall to happen again. As a result, the next time the sequence came up in training, Chloe was reluctant. But her coach yelled out, "Let's go!" So she did it, but it didn't feel very good, and it wasn't very good. That poor result just added fuel to the fire, to the thoughts, the beliefs, and ultimately the fear. The next time Chloe was set to do the sequence, she started out, did her round-off, then back handspring and then she stopped. When her coach urged her to do the back tuck on its own, she succeeded. But Chloe's thinking was aimed at the difficulty she was having completing the sequence, which derailed her to the point where eventually, she stopped trying it at all.

Chloe genuinely believed there was something wrong with her. So what did I do? I helped Chloe to become aware of her thinking patterns and recognize her fear of failure. When I challenged her thinking around injury and embarrassment, she began to realize that none of what she was worried about had happened in reality. This realization helped, but she still wasn't quite there yet. The truth of the matter was no one had stolen the athletic ability out of her body; it was her mind that was quitting on her by telling her she couldn't do it. And guess what? She couldn't do it. Remember, the ones who say they can and the ones who say they can't are both usually right.

For the next few weeks, I asked Chloe to start practicing the sequence on a mat with a spotter, instead of alone on the floor. This way, she had a perceived safety net. And lo and behold, Chloe could do it. Next, I asked her to drop one jelly bean into a jar every time she was able to complete the sequence. Not surprisingly, I didn't get a lot of push back on that exercise. After a couple of weeks, that jar was starting to fill up. At that point, I asked Chloe if she would feel comfortable removing the mat to do the sequence, with her spotter there. She agreed. Then I told her she could put two jelly beans into the jar for every time she executed the sequence without the mat. One week later, Chloe's jar was halfway full. I then asked her if it would be okay to let the spotter determine whether or not she needed to step in for the spot. If the spotter thought Chloe needed the support, she would be right there to help her. If all looked good, she would let things flow naturally. Chloe hesitated a little, but she agreed to try it. I told her that she could put three jelly beans in the jar for every time she completed her sequence this new way. I got a big smile for that one.

Finally, Chloe told me that her jar was full and asked what to do next. "Wow," I said. "You filled that jar pretty quickly. How did you do that?"

She answered that she did it by doing the sequence a lot of times, just like we had discussed.

"So, what do you think that means?" I asked.

She looked at me, smiled and said simply, "I can do it."

Chloe returned to training the next day and, on her own, asked her coach to step away. She was ready to try that sequence on the floor without a spotter. She went for it, and she succeeded.

At the conscious level, giving up is not what anyone really wants to do. Yet, there are times in everyone's life when they have felt like quitting, whether consciously or unconsciously—and that's okay. It happens. You may be okay at times, you may be triggered at times, but every time that underlying fear of failure rears its ugly head, it will drag you down. And every time you respond to failure in a negative way, you disable your ability to move forward. So, if we know that failure in life is unavoidable, the question becomes, how will you choose to look at it, and what are you going to do about it?

In the face of adversity, are you good at convincing yourself that it's not what you really wanted in the first place? Do you blame others so you don't have to admit to yourself that you are giving up? Or, do you use challenge to drive you harder? When you make a mistake on the ice or playing field, at school, or in the boardroom, do you beat yourself up for it and lose drive and motivation? Or do you learn from failure and give it another go? In answering these questions, consider your own adversities, mistakes, fears, and failures, and decide how you want to respond to them in the future. You can make a new choice right now, rather than returning to your automatic reactions. It's easier sometimes in the moment to give up, change course, and not face your fears. But know that those moments are your opportunity to choose whether you grow or stop growing.

"The temptation to quit is usually the strongest just before you are about to succeed." – **Chinese Proverb**

People tend to have a natural instinct to protect themselves from pain, which makes it easy to retreat when faced with adversity. There is definitely an initial gain when one gives up, gives in, or avoids facing fears. In that instant, you feel better because you have protected yourself from immediate fear, pain and disappointment. The problem is, you then set yourself up for more pain in the future. Eventually, you will feel the even greater pain of not being able to move forward to achieve your goals and dreams. I use the following statements with my athletes and business clients to help them identify and work through these situations.

Tagline: *Short-term gain for long-term pain.*

When you take shortcuts, back down, or give up, you are taking that initial gain, but you are setting yourself up for more trouble in the future. What you need to do is learn how to flip that statement around.

Tagline: *Short-term pain for long-term gain.*

Yes, it will be harder and more painful to face fear and difficulty at first. But when you are willing and able to suffer through pain in the short-term, you can and will begin to create your greatest self. If success was easy, then everyone would be doing it.

MISTAKES = LEARNING OPPORTUNITIES

By now, you have learned to acknowledge and accept the fact that failure and mistakes are part of life and part of the pathway to success, especially when you try new things and venture into new territories. So let's learn how to use failure as opportunity. Whether the mistake you make is on a large or small scale, let's figure out how to handle it more productively.

The strategy below will help you let go of the fear of failure. To do that, you have to learn to reframe failure.

Strategy: Reframing Failure Step by Step

1. Answer this question: What do you think about failure?
At this point, you should have a new view of failure as something that is part of life and essential to greatness and success.

2. Develop a mess-up plan.
Have a plan in place so you know what to do and how you will handle situations when they go wrong.

3. Choose your response to the situation.
Consider how you will choose to think about mistakes when they happen.

4. Find a bright side.
Look at your situation and push yourself to find something positive from it.

5. Look for the lesson.
Ask yourself what you can learn from the situation that you can use the next time.

6. Put the lesson into action.

Figure out how you are going to use what happened to make you better.

7. Keep things in perspective.
We often blow our mistakes and failures out of proportion. Put the situation back into perspective. It may feel bad, but it may not be as bad as you think.

8. Shift perspective.
Shift your focus away from the mistake to something more productive, such as thinking about something that may have gone right, or acknowledging that things could have been worse.

9. Choose your focus.
Make a purposeful effort to choose a more productive place to put your focus. Shift from negatives to positives, or to a focus on things you can control.

10. Use the W.I.N statement (What's Important Now?)
Think about what is important right now to help you regroup and refocus.

I remember having one of those days when my schedule was so busy that I had a hard time figuring out how to fit it all in. I prepared by setting up my plan the night before because time was tight and everything needed to run like clockwork. My two sons, Brendan and Noah, had to be dropped off at different locations in the morning, so I asked them to be ready to leave the house at 7:20 a.m. SHARP. Brendan was heading to school and Noah to the hockey rink, where he was set to start his first paid job helping on the ice for a big tryout. Then I had to make it to a 9:00 a.m. lawyer's appointment, followed by a jam-packed schedule of back-to-back appointments and meetings. We had made breakfast and packed lunches and snacks. The school and hockey bags were ready at the front door. We all knew the schedule, set the alarms, and were set to follow the plan.

We got off to a great start and we were all in the car on time. The first drop-off went exactly as planned. There was some traffic ahead, I was feeling tense and watching the clock, but we were on track. As I turned the corner to the rink, I saw a virtually empty parking lot and thought, *Oh CRAP, something is wrong.* And then it hit me: We were at the wrong rink. There it was, my big mistake. I had incorrectly assumed the tryout was at a particular rink, and now my son would be late on the first day of his first job. Worse, I didn't even know where he needed to be. Plus, I was going to be late, and I would never make it through all those carefully planned appointments. The day I had prepared for so well was turning into a mess.

At this stage, there was nothing left to do but follow a new plan, one that would help me reframe the failure and make the most of my day. Here's what I did:

Step 1 - What did I think of failure?
I acknowledged my error then reminded myself that *sh*t happens.*

Step 2 - What was my mess-up plan?
Together, my son and I each created a plan. He called someone to find out the correct destination and I figured out which appointments I could reasonably reschedule.

Step 3 - How did I respond to the situation?
I was feeling pretty bad about things, so I reminded myself that everyone makes mistakes. I also recognized that I was trying to do too many things at one time. I needed to cut myself some slack. What was done was done.

Step 4 - Where did I find the bright side?

I realized that the pressure of the day had been making me feel very stressed, and now, I was forced to lighten up a little.

Step 5 - Where was my lesson?

My lesson was in acknowledging that as usual, I was doing too much. I had put myself under a great deal of stress and I needed to accept that life does not always go exactly as planned.

Step 6 - How did I put my lesson into action?

This one is still a work in progress, but from this experience, I make a conscious effort to create a manageable work schedule, by fitting in breaks so I can recharge throughout the day.

Step 7 - Where was the perspective?

I put the situation back into perspective by reminding myself that the world wouldn't end just because my son or I arrived late. He would still get on the ice, and I have strong enough relationships with my clients that I can always reschedule.

Step 8 - How did I shift perspective?

Doing Step 7 helped me gain a new perspective on the situation. Next, I reminded myself that things could always be much worse, so I would take what I've got. And that felt better.

Step 9 - Where did I choose to focus?

I chose not to keep my focus on how I messed up, but rather on moving forward through the day.

Step 10 - What was important now?

All of the above steps allowed me to move into action. What was important now (W.I.N) was making the necessary calls to reorganize the day so I could live it and enjoy it.

And that was that. My son worked his first job. I got to the lawyer's office where they managed to fit me in. I made it to work and helped my clients, and that's the way the day moved on. It wasn't great, but the truth is, it was okay.

FAIL FORWARD

There is always one session with my athletes and clients where I freak them out a little. They walk into my office and with a big smile on my face, I tell them: *Today we are going to learn how to fail.* They look at me like I am crazy. Some have even asked me, *Why would we do that?! I am here because I don't want to fail.* Other times, when athletes tell me they are upset because they lost, played badly, didn't get played, or whatever else, I tell them I am sorry they are having a hard time, but I am also appreciative that this happened. Again, they think I have lost my mind. I explain to them that there is good news in all of this upset because it has given us the opportunity to talk about it. And since they have survived whatever it is they are dealing with—they didn't crumble or fade away—we can now do something about it. We can work with their failure to develop their mental toughness. We can use this opportunity to learn from and do better. All of this pain is useful because it will ultimately make them stronger, and for that, I am grateful. Then comes that softer, more pensive look that says: *Hmmm, wow. I guess I never really thought of it that way.* And so the learning begins.

From here, we practice going through the steps to reframe their failure or adversity and practice how to fail better so we can move into forward progress. Amazingly, failure, while no one has to like it, gets transformed into a catalyst for growth and therefore much less feared. Of course, I do not promote failure per se, but I do discourage *fear of failure.* Here is another great little tagline I use that helps people to keep going when they feel frozen in the face of their failures or situations gone wrong.

Tagline: *Don't get stuck in the suck. Find an opportunity and move on.*

The reality is that sometimes in sport, at work, in life, or in our families, things suck! It just is what it is. You have a choice, though. You can choose to get stuck in the suck, or you can find an opportunity. So, post this little saying somewhere and use it when things suck. Remind yourself about it. Teach it to your friends and family. Soon you will see that everyone will start using it. It will help keep you on track and you can use it to help others when they fall off track as well. Speaking of which, I have a confession. In my story above about my wrong rink mistake, I left out one important piece of information. Before I moved through those beautiful reframing steps, I was freaking out, stressing out, and feeling awful. It was my son who turned to me and called me out.

"Mom," he said calmly as I stared at him, red-faced and furious. He shook his head and said, "Come on, what is it that you teach me? Don't get stuck in the suck." He got me!

Those few words pack a lot of punch. They snapped me right back into gear. As soon as I heard that magical little phrase, I was able to recognize what I was doing and then move through the reframing steps and carry on. There were other positive takeaways, as well. First, I realized that even though my kids pretend not to listen to me, apparently, they actually do hear what I have to say. Also, there was my proud mom moment, that warm feeling you get when your child handles a situation exactly the way you've taught him.

In the grand scheme of life, my slip-up wasn't monumental. Of course, there are varying degrees of mistakes, failures, and adversities, though. Consider the next case.

"This is all wrong," said the President of the United States of

America while staring at Marc Thiessen who, for the first time, was the chief speechwriter for President George Bush's address. It was June 27, 2005, and the president was to deliver the speech to the nation in less than 24 hours. As Bush tore apart the draft, Marc should have been rattled. After all, his job was on the line. But instead of getting anxious, he somehow went into action mode. He began taking notes while the president pointed out why he was unhappy with the draft and outlined the changes he wanted made. Marc went back to his office, ordered sandwiches and created a game plan. Instead of falling apart, he led himself and chief speechwriter Bill McGurn through an all-nighter where they focused on how to execute the necessary changes. At 5:00 a.m., a new draft was sent to the president.

Marc sat waiting in his office with anticipation when, at 6:45 a.m., the phone rang. He glanced over at the caller ID and saw the letters POTUS flash across the screen. He took a deep breath and picked up the phone to hear these words: "Marc, it's the President. This is much better." Marc let out a sigh of relief. The speech went off that day as planned and was well received.

At the end of that evening, they all flew back to Washington on Air Force One. The president called Marc and Bill into his cabin and said, "Good job, lads. A little rough getting there, but good job." He spoke with a chuckle as he shook their hands.

But the best part of the story was when Marc told me how Bill came to him the next day and asked him how he had managed to stay so calm and to stop himself from buckling under the pressure. Marc's answer was priceless—at least to me.

"Simple," he said, "I was a goalie." Marc explained that by spending so much time on the ice between the pipes growing up, he became used to being the last line of defense. He learned through his hockey experience not to be intimidated by situations where he was "the only thing standing between success and failure."

I love this story and Marc's incredible composure while responding to a high-pressure situation. Marc managed to do so many things necessary to generate a successful outcome. First and foremost, he believed in himself. He listened to the president, took notes, and believed that he could fix whatever wasn't working. He did not focus on the pressure, the timeline, or the potential to lose his job; he focused on the process of creating a favourable outcome. On the spot, he prepared a game plan and an approach to executing it. Marc Theissen created his success that evening. He *failed forward*.

So, here's the lesson: From small mistakes to big ones, from minor setbacks to major ones, just start failing forward. Failure can often be a key ingredient of success, so instead of fearing failure, use a failed situation to learn, grow and try again, until you create the outcome you want.

Here are some fun facts about some impressive people, along with their own words about setbacks and failures. These people all reached high levels of success, but it was not without struggles along the way. Be it in the sports world, the business world, the arts world, the education or political system, Hollywood or anywhere else, there are countless stories of failure behind success.

1. She was fired from her job and told she was not fit for television. Today she is a billionaire and speaks openly about failure and success.

"Failure is another stepping stone to greatness."
– Oprah Winfrey, Talk Show Host, Activist, Actress

2. He had bad grades in high school and was rejected from film school at the University of Southern California multiple times. His perseverance eventually landed him an acceptance to col-

lege and he is now considered to be one the most influential filmmakers of all time.

> *"All good ideas start out with bad ideas. That's why it takes so long."*
> **– Steven Spielberg, Hollywood Producer, Director, Filmmaker**

3. He was pushed out and fired from the very same company he started.

> *"I didn't see it then, but getting fired was the best thing that ever happened to me."*
> **– Steve Jobs, Co-founder and former CEO of Apple**

4. He failed in business, had a nervous breakdown, and was defeated in several elections.

> *"My great concern is not whether you have failed, but whether you are content with your failure."*
> **– Abraham Lincoln, 16th President of the United States of America**

5. He was unsuccessful in school, had a failed attempt at joining the army, failed at an early business venture, which ended up going bankrupt, and was fired from a newspaper for lack of creativity.

> *"We don't look backwards for very long. We keep moving forward, opening up new doors, and doing new things, because we're curious...and curiosity keeps leading us down new paths."*
> **– Walt Disney, Creator of Disney**

CHAPTER 6

MOTIVATION & WORK ETHIC

DON'T WISH FOR IT; WORK FOR IT!

It is clear that success and greatness come from the ability to push through failures and fear of failure. Now it's time to acknowledge that at the end of the day, you don't get what you wish for, but rather, you get what you work for. I often hear people talking about all of the things they want to achieve and accomplish. But talk is just talk. If I watched you day in and day out, would I SEE what it is you are working for? Would I see by your day-to-day actions and behaviours exactly what it is you want? Answer that question honestly, without excuses like *I didn't get the chance, I don't have the time,* or *My coach, teacher, boss, colleague, business partner, etc. is not treating me right.*

It's easy to make excuses, blame others, or let life's circumstances get in the way of pursuing your dreams. Sometimes we buy into our own excuses, believing them to be the truth, and other times, there really are hard realities in our way. You may in fact be getting the short end of every stick. You may not have the right support. But whether this adversity is based in reality or on excuses, it doesn't matter. It is your job to take control and create the life you want. You may encounter people who don't want you to get ahead, or who don't like you. There may be major things going on in your life that are genuinely difficult, or you may just be your own worst enemy. So, what is it? You must begin to identify the stumbling blocks in order to move past them. No one can do that work for you.

I said earlier that greatness takes time, and it does. But it also takes work. Those who achieve great and long-term success are willing to work for it, period. So, now is the time to stop being fearful, making excuses, blaming others and allowing life to get in the way. Instead, deliberately use failure to fuel you and make you stronger. When things suck, which they often will in life, you have a choice. You can let your circumstances get you down, or you can do the work to move forward in spite of them. That's known as drawing upon your resilience—or grit. It's your ability to go out and get what you want, regardless of your current positioning, family situation, finances, or life state. What you achieve is going to be a direct representation of how you think and how you behave. So get the mindset right and get to work. Show me your grit.

Target Thought: *A goal without action is just a wish.*

I spent a few years teaching and running a sport psychology program at a specialized high school for elite athletes. These athletes had the unique opportunity to combine their academics and athletics during the school day in order to further pursue their dreams within sport. One of the first things I told my students is that it's often the character they exhibit through their behaviour in class and in their day-to-day lives, not just their talent, that allows me to predict how far they will go in their sport.

The interest level from the kids in this class ranged from being intrigued to impassive, to some who showed no interest at all. Over the years, I reminded myself that these athletes were in the class because it was part of their program, not because they chose to take it. So, I would set my own little challenge, which was to try and engage them all, including those who would have preferred to be anywhere else. I worked hard to get my messages across in a fun, creative and enticing way, and I could usually win over the group. One year however, there was a particularly challenging class with a couple of boys I won't soon forget. These boys, we'll call them Jayden and Daniel, clearly had no interest in being there. I didn't take it personally, as they seemed to have no interest in doing anything other than being on the ice or hanging out with their friends. But I was still up for the challenge of trying to engage them.

Unfortunately, though, Jayden and Daniel most often skipped the class. When they did appear in their seats, they came across as rude, arrogant, and often disrespectful. At the time, they were both top OHL draft picks, and were banking on hockey for their future. Day by day, when they did show up, I tried my best to engage them. I even brought in hula hoops to incorporate into a cool mental game activity, getting them up and out of their seats for some fun. I split the students into two groups and asked them to gather around the hula hoops and hold them up with one finger. Everyone in the class got up to secure a spot around the hula hoop, except for Daniel. He couldn't even bother to stand. I was dumbfounded by the disrespect and asked if he would be joining us. He looked up at me, shrugged his shoulders, shook his head and grunted, *Nah.* I told him I could see he had no interest in being there and I didn't want to waste his time, and then I asked him to leave the class. Wow, I had never done that before. I had never needed to.

During the next class, I deliberately chose to cover the topic of character and the role it plays in achieving success in sport, along with the value it holds for scouts in their selection process. I thought maybe, just maybe, this information might wake these guys up. Then I spoke about recognizing how actions and behaviours, both on and off the ice, need to match the goals they are working to reach. I shared stories of talented NHL players who destroyed their careers due to their lack of character and stories of other players who made their careers based on good character. I expressed concern that there may be players in this room who could be headed down that same road of sabotaging their opportunities for success by showing a lack of character and work ethic off the ice.

For boys like Jayden and Daniel, listening in my class, or any classes, seemed unimportant, as they were used to getting by with preferential treatment because of how gifted they were on the ice. Come to think of it, they didn't even have to work that hard on the ice, since their natural talent and skill made it easy for them to dominate the game. In fact, because they were ranked as top upcoming prospects, everyone around them worked to make things easy for them. Why work hard in school when they were essentially being handed passing grades anyway?

Jayden and Daniel did have plans of their own, however. Daniel was going to pursue the OHL route, while Jayden, who wanted to follow the NCAA route, had been getting Division 1 College scholarship offers since tenth grade. Jayden was able to choose one of the best schools with one of the best hockey programs, and for a couple of years, all went exactly as planned. Then he started college, and life as he knew it changed. All of a sudden, no one was catering to him anymore. In school, he was expected to work for his grades like everyone else if he wanted to get by. On the ice, he became one of many great hockey players out there. For Jayden, this change was a real wake up call. He had been so used to everything coming easily to him, everyone helping him and pushing him through, that he never learned to work for what he wanted. He had gotten by purely on natural talent, but eventually, talent alone runs out. Without the willingness to work hard for what you want, you simply won't succeed in the long run.

Today, Jayden is still working to figure it all out. This highly ranked prospect who excited everyone just a few years back has seemed to fall off the radar. His NHL draft year came and went and his name was not called. Unfortunately, it looks like my call about how he carried himself off the ice is proving to be true. It is a real shame to see such genuine talent wasted. It is my hope, though, that he will use his current struggles as a lesson to power him forward and reach success. If he can learn to work for it as hard as he wants it, the possibilities could be endless.

I'm sad to say that I was never able to follow up with these two boys, but the good news is, I have used the situation to evaluate how I can improve my own teaching approach with challenging students. The next year, I was lucky enough to have a couple more students just like them in my class, so I got the chance to try it all over again. This time, I did things differently, by spending some one on one time with the challenging guys instead of trying to reach them in a classroom setting. The individual meetings took time but they were worth it. The students came unwillingly in the beginning, but eventually, I was able to connect with them, and their behaviour in class improved. In the end, I have to view my challenge with Jayden and Daniel as the valuable learning experience it was. We all have to put in constant and consistent effort in order to become great at what we do.

"With few exceptions, the best players are usually the hardest workers."
– Magic Johnson, Basketball Icon

GET CLEAR

Another big hurdle for many people is mustering up and sustaining the motivation and drive, day in and day out, to do the hard work that it takes to be successful. It's difficult to be motivated to do something if you don't know exactly what it is you want. So, first, you have to engage in some introspection and become clear on what it is you want to achieve and why.

Too many people lack commitment to their work not only because they are afraid to fail, but also because they are in it for the wrong reasons, they are unclear about their goals, or they fail to identify and connect to the action steps it takes to reach them. To that end, let's work to gain some clarity. If I ask you right now what it is you want, can you very clearly answer that question? Don't be afraid to throw it out there, whatever it is, as long as you are willing to back it up with the action required to make it happen. So, what do you want? If you can't come up with an answer, ask yourself why not. I am guessing that there is still some fear underneath there somewhere.

Once you can clearly articulate what you want, you need to take a good, hard look in the mirror. No excuses, no bullshit. You've got to be honest with yourself about your current level of overall functioning within your field, sport, or life situation, so you can be clear on how to build from there. The first step is to note those main tasks and skills required to successfully get the job done. For example, let's assume you would like to play in the NHL. I have worked closely enough with an NHL scout to tell you the main points used in evaluating players. On ice, he is looking for expertise in the areas of skating skills, puck skills, hockey sense, shooting, compete level, strength, work ethic, or as he described it, how well their 'engine' runs. Off the ice, considerations tend to relate to character and the type of person you show yourself to be.

Athlete or not, there are tasks and skills required for you to be "in the game" in terms of what it is you want. You need knowledge, a necessary skill set, and certain character traits, such as grit, solid values, leadership skills, and a strong work ethic, to win at your game—whether that's in the corporate boardroom, at school, at home or in your personal playing field. Use the following exercise to evaluate yourself and gain clarity with respect to your current status and what you need to do to reach your goals.

Self-Evaluation Exercise Part 1: Discover where you are and where you need to be.

Identify the main tasks and skills required to get to where you want to be. Next, put a checkmark in the appropriate box beside the skill that best describes your current performance level within that field. You will then clearly see where you need to focus your attention. From there, figure out the action steps required to make improvements.

E = Exceed the basic/average level required
M = Meet the basic/average level required
B = Fall below the basic/average level required

If you are unsure of the required skill set because you are venturing into a new area, then your first task is to do your research. Check reliable sources to learn what it takes to succeed in the field so you have a framework to start with.

TASKS/SKILLS	E – EXCEED	M – MEET	B– BELOW

It is helpful to delve even further and really get to know yourself. Consider the unique traits you either bring to the table or may be lacking, such as coachability, sportsmanship, ability to be a team player, leadership qualities, presence in a room, ability to set boundaries and take risks, mindset, learning styles, decision making, handling conflict, and so on. To help you gain a deeper level of insight and self-knowledge, use the list of questions below, which I developed for NHL scouts in their interviewing process for the NHL draft selection. They were designed to help uncover the person behind the equipment, in order to better assist in player selections. Regardless of whether or not you are an athlete, you can use these questions to gain clarity into what makes you tick. Take your time and think about your answers, and most importantly, be honest.

Self-Evaluation Exercise Part 2: Get in touch with who you are.

1. What is one word you would use to best describe yourself?
2. What are your best personality traits?
3. What are your worst personality traits?
4. How do others see you? How would they describe you?
5. What do you think about mistakes and failure?
6. If you are given a new task, do you jump right in, or do you take time to gather information and figure out how you are going to approach it?
7. How have you gotten to where you are now? What do you attribute your success (or struggles) to?
8. If you could change one thing about yourself, what would it be?
9. What are qualities you admire in others?
10. What is your greatest fear and why?

INTRINSIC VERSUS EXTRINSIC MOTIVATION

With clarity, we can begin to evaluate where personal motivation is rooted. There are many different theories around motivation, but what is most important is to be able to recognize and understand your own motivational drives and what propels you to action. If you know what the underlying push is that motivates you to behave, you can check in to see if the drive is in line with your goals and is helping to increase or decrease your overall motivation. Ask yourself: Are you currently being motivated by intrinsic or extrinsic factors? Let me explain.

Intrinsic motivation is doing something because you choose it, because you find it interesting, enjoyable, and/or personally rewarding. *Extrinsic motivation,* on the other hand, is when you are motivated by external factors such as a reward like money, social approval and recognition, or the avoidance of negative consequences or punishment. While both types of motivations can mobilize you into action, the most rewarding and long-lasting is intrinsic motivation. Keep in mind that these two drives can often become intertwined. For example, it can be highly motivating to make a lot of money and gain recognition. At the same time however, being connected to what you love, and pursuing your passion is what most often enables you to achieve that money/recognition.

Intrinsic motivation helps you to honour the sacrifices you make to do what you do, and to withstand the adversity you face along the way. It helps you find fulfillment and happiness in both your journey toward and within your success. On the flip side, when you are driven solely by extrinsic factors, you are likely to lose satisfaction along the way, leaving you always needing more, because you are never truly fulfilled deep down inside. Consider the person who has all the money in the world, but is miserable. A sense of autonomy, competence and relatedness are basic psychological needs and satisfying those needs helps to fuel intrinsic motivation, thus facilitating and maintaining longer-lasting motivation.

A former NHL player we'll call Dave once told me that throughout his playing career, he was driven to win the Stanley Cup. "That's what it's all about," he told me, even though after a solid 11-season career in the NHL, he had never won a Stanley Cup. In an attempt to share my theories on motivation, I questioned him further but he was having none of it.

"What else is there? That's why we play. That's what it's all about," he said. Yes, the Stanley Cup is a pretty big deal! Still, I was struggling with his perspective. How many hockey players even get to the NHL level, and of those, how many actually win the Stanley Cup? Very few. Does that mean that all of the rest haven't been successful, are left unfulfilled, or have lost motivation along the way?

After analyzing further, I got a better sense of what motivated Dave. As I listened to his stories and watched him as he spoke about his hockey days, I realized that he really was driven to play for all the right reasons because I could feel his passion for the game. It was evident that playing hockey at the NHL level gave him a real sense of personal achievement and autonomy. He also played because he loved playing. It filled his need for competence, a personal sense of effectiveness and the need for relatedness one gets from belonging to something special. Still today, some 20 or so years later, he recalls his playing days with a spark in his eyes. He was smiling and enjoying sharing his story about being part of The Heritage Classic in Winnipeg, featuring the infamous Winnipeg Jets vs Edmonton Oilers matchup of the '80s. He still belongs to the hockey world and he still has a love for the game and everything it stands for.

So yes, he pushed himself to win a Stanley Cup, but it wasn't just the trophy that motivated him. His love of the game is what got him out of bed every morning, ready to work hard. Hockey was a part of him, then and now. So, the answer is no, he is not left unfulfilled because he never achieved the Stanley Cup dream. He is accomplished and successful because he played the game for all the right reasons. For the love of the game. And the more connected you are to that love for what you do, the greater your overall satisfaction and ultimate success will be.

What is driving you right now? Is that the right motivating factor for you? If not, what is getting in the way of finding your intrinsic motivation? Here are some more good questions to ask yourself:

1. What do you love to do?
2. What puts a smile on your face when you do it?
3. What activities make you feel good?

If no easy answers come to you, then go back to a time in your life when you remember being happy and fulfilled. What were you doing? Tell me this: If you had one real wish to do anything in the world right now, what would it be? That's what you need to start working on.

STUMBLING BLOCKS

With your newfound clarity and insights, you can pinpoint what may be holding you back. Are you too worried about what others will think? Are you too focused on making money, on avoiding failure, or on the need to be recognized or admired? Are you too worried about letting others down? Did you not realize it would be so hard? Would you rather sit on the couch, watch TV, or play video games? Did you make a mistake you think you can't rectify? Are you worried it's too late?

There will always be obstacles in the way, whether they come from within you or from external forces. Your job is to recognize those obstacles so you can choose the right thoughts and interpretations around them. You have to look head-on at each stumbling block—whether that's a fear, a situation or circumstances—and then be willing to battle it. This process will propel you toward positive action. Your motivation to succeed will increase when your purpose and passion become greater than your fear and your distractions.

If what you are working for is truly worthwhile, do not expect an easy journey. A wise man once told me that if it's too good to be true then it's probably too good to be true. People often picture success as a steady climb, but in reality, it is full of ups and downs, and twists and turns. Make sure you know that, and be willing to tackle them so you can forge ahead.

Motivational Insight Exercise: Assess your level of drive.

- Rank your current motivation level on a scale of 1 to 10.
- What stops you from being a 10?
- Are you intrinsically or extrinsically motivated?
- Is what you want worth it to you?
- Do your actions and behaviours match what you are working for?

I engaged in a powerful exercise at a sport psychology conference I once attended. Its purpose was to help athletes and teams recognize if they were doing the right things to achieve their desired goals, or if they were just kidding themselves. Not only was this exercise fun, but it also facilitated one of those *AHA!* moments that give us great insight without explanation.

We learned how to run this exercise in a team environment, using a jug of water and many cups. The team captain, standing in the middle of the room surrounded by teammates, had to state the team's goal. Together, members of the team wrote down each of the tasks they deemed necessary to achieving their goal on individual cue cards and placed each one in front of a corresponding cup. The captain was then asked to think about all of the activities the players on the team do in a day, like practice, train, attend school, hang out with friends, play video games, etc. and add each activity to a new cue card and corresponding cup. Once the cups and cards were all set, the fun began.

The captain was handed the jug with a set amount of water in it, symbolizing time commitment. The task was to fill each cup to the level they felt their team committed their time to. For example, if they spent 10% of their time hanging out with friends, they would pour 10% of the water from the jug into the friend's cup. They could play around with the water and adjust it among the cups until they felt it was an accurate representation of how they spent their time. The teammates were there to challenge the captain and to hold one another accountable for honesty.

Once the team was finished, they were asked to decide if they wanted to make any final adjustments. Then came the big challenge. They had to take a good hard look at the water levels in the cups and think about where the water actually *needs* to be in order to achieve their stated goal and ask the question: *Is it in the right places?* At that point, the team was given another opportunity to make adjustments, but only with the current amount of water. Why? They were told that there is only a limited amount of time in a day, so it was up to them to decide how to redistribute the water most effectively. *AHA!* This is where the players realized that there was too much water in the video games cup and not enough time in individual training. They recognized that there was not very much time in their family time cup, yet they need and rely on family support to help them with their goals. And so on.

Excited about the results, I rushed home to try this exercise with my sons. Would it generate the same impact on them? Teenage boys were my test before I used it in my practice. It was entertaining to watch them at work. My sons had to think carefully about how to move the water around. It was very clear that they had plenty of water in their TV watching and video games cups, but not enough in their studying, working out and homework cups. So, they set off on their mission to move the water into the appropriate places, because they knew those cups were not full enough to achieve their goals. It was hard to decide what to give up. Without me saying a word, they giggled and gave me a *You got me!* look.

If they got it, you can too, by trying this exercise. It will help you rethink what you need to do, practically, to move toward achieving your goals.

Time Juggle Exercise: Allot the right amount of time to your goals.

Follow the steps in the story above, identifying the necessary time components involved for you in your life and in achieving your goals.

- If you have a goal around athletics, is your water in the right cups?
- If your goal is to start a new business, is your water in the right cups?
- If you want to be a good coach, parent or teacher, is your water in the right cups?

Try it and see what you come up with!

GET ALL IN

Chapter by chapter, you are developing your mindset, reframing failure, controlling the controllables, building your confidence, identifying your passions, recognizing your fears and accepting the bumpy road to success. Keep working on each of them, and particularly any that you have identified as stumbling blocks. So what now? Now it's time to go all in. Commit to climbing your way up to number 10 on your personal motivation scale because it's time to go from good to great.

A young man set out on a journey of self-discovery. Through his travels, he came upon a dense forest. He needed to get across to the other side, but the trees were thick and the forest looked dark. He stopped to think. He wasn't sure how to get through. He looked around, but could not seem to move forward. While his body felt frozen in place and his eyes scanned across the forest, he noticed a footpath on the far left side. He was automatically set into motion and headed straight toward it. *Thank goodness*, he thought, *there is an easy way to get across the forest.* As he looked at the pathway in front of him, a small voice inside his head spoke to him: *I get why you want to take the path. It appears to be the logical thing to do. It is the path of least resistance, the easier way to go. But are you sure that is what you want to do?*

Right then, he understood. His journey was about self-discovery. It was not about traveling the same old paths, but about discovering new ones. This particular footpath had been created by millions of footsteps walking on it back and forth, forth and back, over and over again. The purpose of this young man's journey was to break through his own barriers and build a new path, not to repeat the old comfortable way of getting somewhere. He took a deep breath, turned away from the pathway and started snapping branches as he crashed his way through the forest. It was tough work. He got scratched and bruised and beat up as he forged his way through the trees, but when he finally emerged into the light, he felt elated. He now knew he could accomplish anything he set his mind to, and he was empowered to try.

Think about those habits and behaviours you have repeated so many times that they have become robotic. These are the pathways we naturally return to over and over again because they come easy to us. What I am asking you to do is to commit to carving a new, more powerful pathway, with new thoughts and new habits. Starting will take some work. You'll need to crash through the forest and walk those steps hundreds of thousands of times. As you move ahead with this process, you will break free from old patterns and barriers that are blocking your path to personal greatness and success.

Reading books is one step toward helping you to understand personal growth, but reading alone will not create long-lasting change. You have to take the steps out there in the world. Just as a new pathway is created in the forest, so too can we build a new pathway in the mind. Let's take a closer look at some of the new footsteps you can start walking, by using the techniques below. They will help you choose new behaviours, increase your motivational drive and keep you moving toward your goals.

WRITE DOWN YOUR GOALS

First and foremost, WRITE DOWN YOUR GOALS. It's a small act, but there is something very powerful about committing your goals to paper. Not only will successful people tell you that doing so helps drive them, but there is also a great amount of research that proves that writing down your goals increases commitment and achievability. How?

When you write down your thoughts, you take them from the abstract and make them tangible. Now you have distinguished your goals from the other countless thoughts that flood your mind on any given day. In addition, having your goals in front of you makes it easier for you to measure your progress and build competence and confidence. The bottom line is, seeing them helps you commit to acting on them. How many New Year's resolutions do you think are spoken on December 31st? And how many of them do you think are actually kept?

Think of your goals like climbing a ladder. At the top of the ladder is your ultimate goal. It's that wonderful aspiration you dream about, which I sometimes refer to as the dream goal, or your long-term goal. Then, back down you go to today, the starting point, or the bottom of the ladder. This is where you set some immediate goals, the things you are going to commit to right now. From there, climb a couple of steps and set short-term goals. These are the targets you would like to hit over the next three months to one year. Then continue climbing the ladder, adding the mid-term goals that you would like to reach over the next one, two or even five years, moving you toward your end point. Finally, there is that long-term goal waiting for you at the top. Depending on what the goal is and how you are doing, you can adjust the targets and the timing that it will take for you to reach it.

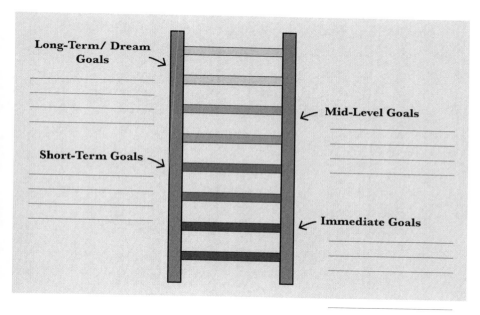

SET SMART GOALS

In order to make sure you are setting meaningful and achievable goals, use what is referred to as S-M-A-R-T goals. They are not only smart, but we use the word as an acronym, with each of the letters representing an attribute essential to building productive goals. They are as follows:

S: *Specific*

Vague goals, such as *I want to be the best*, are not good goals. Make sure when you write down your goals they are specific, such as *I would like to win a specified award, get drafted, or be nominated for the Top 30 under 30.*

M: *Measurable*

You have to be able to measure your progress in a specific way. Some goals have built-in ways to measure achievement, such as getting drafted, while others do not. It is important to always make sure you have a way to quantify your progress, for example, by devising a tracking chart to monitor achievement as you take the steps to reach your goal.

A: *Attainable and Action Steps*

Be certain that what you want to achieve is attainable. For instance, if you want to reach the goal of bench pressing a certain amount, then you will first need access to weights. Next, outline the action steps you will follow in order to achieve each one of your goals. For instance: *I will go to the gym four times a week.*

R: *Realistic*

We want our goals to be challenging and to push us, but at the same time, they need to be realistic. Otherwise, you are setting yourself up for failure. You don't have to take an unrealistic goal off the table but rather, break it down into more realistic stages and measure progress along the way. Once you have made considerable development and the ultimate goal is no longer out of reach, then you bring it back into the mix.

T: *Timely*

Be sure to set a timeline with target dates for when you will set out to accomplish each goal. You can also set shorter target dates to measure and check in on your progress along the way. This way, you can determine if you are on track or falling short, and see what adjustments need to be made.

Targeting end results is a necessary part of the goal setting process. By consciously setting out the result you want to achieve, you will know what you are working toward. Then you can outline the action steps and set timelines for evaluation. This framework is very different from driving yourself with a result-oriented focus on a daily basis—with expectations. There is no judgment when you are setting goals. You are simply setting yourself confidently on a path, with a plan and a timeline, rather than getting dizzy on a daily emotional rollercoaster and being reactive with your confidence.

SPEAK IT OUT LOUD

When you say a goal out loud, you enhance your commitment to it. Here's a fascinating story. In 1961, John F. Kennedy announced to the world that he would put a man safely on the moon by the end of the decade. *Yeah right*, people thought. But on July 20, 1969, Neil Armstrong took his first step on the moon. JFK said it, and he did it. Around that time as well, there was a major league baseball player who played for the San Francisco Giants named Gaylord Perry. Perry was a pitcher who had a lengthy and successful career in Major League Baseball. He was a five-time All-star, winner of the Cy Young award for best pitcher in the MLB, and was elected into the Baseball Hall of Fame in 1991. While Perry's pitching skills were impressive, his hitting ability never quite measured up. We can't be great at everything.

In 1963, Perry was confronted with some chirping about his inability to hit, and he owned it. There is some controversy as to who said it, either Perry or his manager, but someone responded that there will be a man on the moon before Perry hits a home run. In a fascinating turn of events, on July 20, 1969, the very same day of the Apollo 11 moon landing and Neil Armstrong's first steps on the moon, Gaylord Perry hit his first home run within hours of the landing.

Saying a goal aloud can increase motivation, commitment and accountability. I guess you could say it gives people that little extra push to make it happen. It sure did for Perry. Throughout his career, that was the first and last home run he ever hit.

CREATE A VISION BOARD

Here's a fun exercise that can help increase motivation to reach your goals: create a board that symbolizes your vision. You can put anything and everything onto this board that inspires you—pictures of role models, artifacts, magazine photos, newspaper clippings, news from the internet. Get as creative as you can. When your board is complete, place or hang it in a spot where you will see it every day when you wake up and when you go to bed. Seeing the vision of what it is you are working for helps reinforce your commitment by keeping you connected to it on a daily basis.

FOLLOW A SCHEDULE

We all know how hectic life can get. If you don't set aside the time to do the tasks you need to do, they will often go undone. So, make yourself a schedule and be sure to allot the necessary time to do the important things you need to do. Then follow it.

When I committed to writing this book, I was excited. I enjoyed the process. Whenever I had free time, I would sit down and write. The problem was, I never had free time. I have a full practice where I spend six days of the week meeting with clients and teams.

At the time, I was also running a new start-up and separate division of my company in my off-hours, and I was booking for speaking engagements, too. I kept saying that when work slowed down, I would get back to the book. But work didn't slow down, and as time went on, I realized I was falling more and more behind. It wasn't that I didn't want to write. I didn't lack the motivation to work hard. I simply could never find the time.

Finally, one day, I sat down with my schedule and I blocked off time for writing. When I looked at my daily calendar, I was able to identify moments of opportunity. I was also able to prioritize and reorganize my commitments, in order to accommodate more time for writing. Doing so enabled me to find the time I needed to achieve my goal.

ESTABLISH GOOD HABITS

Aristotle once said, "We are what we repeatedly do." That means we have to develop purposeful and strong behaviours to back up what it is we want. We also need good habits in place to support the learning we have done with respect to our thinking and our fearless approach to producing our own greatness. One of the best ways to begin doing this is to build behavioural chains. Instead of re-inventing the wheel, you can simply build upon the regular behaviours and routines you already practice every day. How?

Highlight the action steps you have pinpointed as central to your success and then fit them into your regular routine. For example, I tell my athletes who want to get stronger to do a certain number of push-ups in the morning as soon as they engage in the regular routine of brushing their teeth. If you would like to foster the growth mindset as a coach, praise the effort you see in your players after the regular routine of a practice or a game. If you want to manage your time better, spend 15 minutes organizing your upcoming day before your routine of going to bed every night. If you want to improve your nutrition, prepare what you are going to eat for lunch before your regular routine of taking a shower the night before. And so on and so on. Build good habits into what you already do and keep on doing them.

SET UP A SELF-DEVELOPMENT PLAN

To help you go all in, use your new understanding of where you are at and what you need to do to effectively pursue your goals and construct a personal self-development plan. Start by identifying the things you would like to develop within yourself. These can be bigger picture things related to self-growth, such as learning how to run a business, networking, managing anxiety, financial planning, or getting better at public speaking. Get the right people and training in place to help you acquire the skills you need for personal advancement, and go get it done. Stay focused on continuous self-development. It's an ongoing and never-ending process.

SURROUND YOURSELF WITH GOOD PEOPLE

The following phrase is a favourite among motivational speakers, philosophers and people in leadership roles: *You are the sum of the five people you spend your time with*. I like this phrase because it's important to surround yourself with good people as you make your way toward personal greatness. There will be many different people who come in and out of your life, some of whom are better influences than others, but all of whom will impact you in some way. In your day-to-day life, I want you to figure out what you can learn from each of them, the good and the bad. When you do have the choice about who to spend your time with, choose good people—those who share the same values as you, have good habits, and can inspire the same in you. Being surrounded by good people, good thinkers, and general positivity rubs off, and of course, the opposite is also true. Make sure you know the difference, and choose your friends wisely.

EAT, SLEEP, MOVE

Proper sleep hygiene is a very important element when it comes to your ability to work hard and stay motivated. When you are tired, it is so much harder to drive yourself toward a goal. Pushing yourself to construct your best self can be hard enough work, so don't add additional obstacles. Follow a consistent sleep schedule to keep your body regulated. That way, you will set yourself up to be ready to take on your day. Also consider fueling your body with healthy nutrition, and getting active. Taking care of your health enables you to feel better, which is part and parcel of being better. Healthy body, healthy mind.

WORK HARD, PLAY HARD

Hard work is obviously essential to achieving success, but believe it or not, so is fitting in fun and down time. It is so important to take time out to recharge, refuel, and create some balance in your life, but making it happen can often be challenging. I know it is for me. I always feel as if my workload prevents me from taking time off. I know I could work around the clock and still not have enough time in the day to get everything done. Hard as it is to do, sometimes, I force myself to shut it down, and make all of my work wait. My husband and kids accuse me of overworking. My parents also express concern, constantly telling me that the body is like a machine. If you don't refuel it, it will break down. I try to remember all of their words when I'm so stressed I can hardly think. That's when I take a break, even if it's only for an hour to rejuvenate.

Many years ago, I had the opportunity to watch a group of soon-to-be doctors approaching their medical school graduation. Saturday night came around, and there was a celebratory party planned. I remember being shocked at how hard these guys partied, well into the wee hours of the night. I wasn't expecting so much fun from a group of keen, Type A personality, medical students. By the time the next morning rolled around however, they were all deep in the books again, studying hard for their exams. Hour after hour, until late into that next night, it was all about libraries and books and studying. Nothing was going to distract them. What a lesson I learned. Work hard—and when you have some time, play hard. And then, get right back at it.

BUILD IN RECOVERY TIME

When you've established a strong focus on hard work and giving it everything you've got, it is important to remember to build in recovery time. After long hours and great sacrifice, athlete or not, be sure to allow your body and mind the appropriate time needed to avoid burnout in order to keep moving forward and continue to be effective. Recovery time is key to high performance sustainability and long term motivation.

CHAPTER 7

DEFINING AND REDEFINING SUCCESS

STAY THE COURSE

What a day heading off to college or university can be! It's the beginning of a whole new journey in one's life. It's also the culmination of a stressful time period, from the daunting application process to the days of shaken nerves as acceptance and rejection letters roll in, to the making of final decisions about a new life direction and where the next number of years will lead. It's an exciting and tumultuous time. I had the privilege to go through the adventure personally and then to experience it again as my son Brendan had his turn. You would think I had all the answers by now but in fact, it was very different to watch this transition happen from the outside.

Brendan struggled to make decisions and find his way. In the end, he chose to veer off from the "norm" and chose a path that was less traveled. When his journey was about to begin, he watched all of his friends pack their belongings, load their cars and head off to school together, away from home. Almost all of them were headed to Western University, or to another popular out-of-town university. For the first time in his life, Brendan was on his own, without his support group of best friends, the people he had gone to school with from the time he was three years old. Now he sat at home, starting to second-guess his decision to commute downtown to Ryerson University's Sport Media program, one of the best in the country. He wondered why he hadn't just joined his friends at Western. But the decision was made and it was time to prepare for his new journey.

Filled with nerves, Brendan headed from his sheltered world in suburbia toward downtown. He found himself alone on a city bus en route to the subway station. Smashed between people, he stumbled to find space on the train to grab hold of a handrail so he wouldn't fall over as it jerked away. Surfacing from underground about an hour and a half later, he stepped onto one of the busiest street corners in Canada, Yonge and Dundas Square. After fighting his way through the crowds, he finally arrived at his new school.

It took a great deal of perseverance just to get this far. He had already fielded all kinds of negative feedback from others: *Sports Media? Are you sure you really want to do that?! It's a new program and they haven't even graduated a class yet. I don't think there are many jobs or very much money in that field, and the chances of making it are slim to none. Do you really think that is a good choice?* Both excited and scared, there he stood, wondering if he had made the right decision. It was a different path from the traditional fields of business, law, medicine or accounting, but it was his chosen path and, at the start, a lonely and somewhat courageous one.

At the first sports media school party, Brendan walked in alone. He was definitely out of his comfort zone. Slowly but surely, he started to make friends. He was introduced to his teachers, his classes and his labs. He enjoyed talking about sports all day, with people who loved sports as much as he did. In time, his trepidation and nerves dwindled and began to turn into excitement and passion. Little by little, Ryerson became a new home. After he wrote his last exam of the year, I asked what he thought of his decision now. He told me he couldn't think of any better place to be. He visits his old friends and anxiously awaits their return home for the summer, but he wouldn't trade his program for anything. He is loving what he is doing and defining his own success, and he couldn't be happier.

DEFINING YOUR OWN SUCCESS

What does success mean to you? What does it look like? If you had to paint a picture of it, what would you see and how would it make you feel? There are so many different definitions of success. We know that people want to be successful. Athletes want to win. Everyone wants to accomplish something. Most people want to make money, gain prestige, be happy, and so on. These are common answers, but don't let society or the people in your life create the definition. Instead, start talking about what success looks like and feels like for you, and how you will know when you have achieved it.

Too often, I hear that success is about winning championships. Now, that's an admirable goal, but the fact is, nobody plays to lose. Everyone wants to win, but at the end of the day, there can only be one winner. And then, there is a new day. So, there has got to be more to success than winning. When I push athletes and coaches on their definitions of success, I hear some amazing answers. I hear about connection, camaraderie and lifelong friendships. I hear about developing a brotherhood, building character, and raising kids into fine, capable adults.

I ask all of my clients about their definition of success. Parents tell me that success is knowing that their child feels loved and protected. Business people talk about doing something that changes the world and impacts lives. Teachers say success is about creating a love of learning. Coaches speak about character and sportsmanship. There is so much more to success than awards, championships, money and prestige. When you find that deeper meaning, driving your success will have a whole new sense of power.

Target Thought & Tagline: *I am the author of my own story.*

KEY INGREDIENTS

So much of creating success is having the right mindset and being clear about what you want and what you need to do to get it. You've got the foundation. You have the tools to develop the right mindset and the confidence. You know how to handle failure and adversity. But what would you identify to be the fundamentals needed to succeed in your recipe for achieving your personal sense of greatness? These are the ingredients that simply cannot be substituted or left out.

If you are an athlete, you could think strength, speed, nutrition, and skill. If you are in the corporate world, think about being a great leader, commanding a strong presence in a room, having notable listening and analytical skills, modeling behaviour, and showing all-round positivity. If you want to be good teacher or coach, then some of your ingredients include getting to know each student/athlete as an individual, using effective communication strategies and being able to communicate messages that your students or athletes can relate to and understand. Successful parenting involves learning about healthy parenting, setting boundaries, spending quality time, expressing love. Ask yourself, based on your own definition of success and what you want to accomplish, what five ingredients would be required?

Main Ingredients Exercise: Break Down Your Success.

1. Identify and write down the five key ingredients you would classify as pivotal to creating personal greatness in your field. What would be the required behaviours, skills, knowledge, experience,

character traits, or anything else you would deem to be of utmost importance in achieving your success?

2. Once you have established these, your job is to start building and finding the resources available to help you attain them and implement them.

LET IT VEIN THROUGH

With your definition of success and key ingredients clear, you want to keep the conversations about success going with yourself, your teammates, your friends, your family, your business partners and your colleagues. Once you've got it down, you want to make sure that you purposely allow it to vein through your day-to-day behaviours and your life. Support your definition of success on a daily basis and attend to your key ingredients using the techniques below to help you.

THE PERSONAL CLEANSE

On the way to personal greatness, we are clearing out fear, negative thinking, and all of the other noise. Another way to clean your slate so you can start fresh and embark upon your new journey is to clean up your living space and your life. We are trying to move with purposeful direction now on that pathway toward success, so let's make sure we start clean. What better way to kick off this new approach than by tidying up your room, your gym or your workspace? Keeping the environment in which you are trying to be productive neat and organized will significantly impact how you work and feel.

Once you've tidied up your space, it's time to tackle your relationships. Maybe you need to make peace with someone, or maybe you need to let go of someone emotionally. Who are the people you spend your time with? Who is supporting you in what you do? Who is sucking the life and energy from you, and taking you away from what you need to accomplish? Who is building you up and who is knocking you down? You need to strip away the people who generate distraction in your life and inhibit your growth and success. This step can be a difficult one, but it is necessary to producing your greatest self.

You may also need to tidy up your finances. Make sure you are knowledgeable about the state of your current financial situation, along with what is working for you and what is not. Take a good hard look at where the money is coming in and where it is going out, and clean up whatever you need to, even if that's just going through your credit card or bank statements and taking note of all of the automatic charges processed. As helpful as technology and automation has become, there can be a downside. You might be surprised by what you are not paying attention to, like how many subscriptions you have and don't use even though they seemed like a smart idea at first. Take note, and clean it up.

NETWORKING

There is a lot to do and think about along the road to success, but if no one knows who you are, then you are going to have a really hard time getting anywhere. As you do the necessary work to build the best version of yourself, you need to foster relationships within your field. Start connecting with the right people, including trainers, mentors, role models and other people who have already achieved the type of success you want. Having those associations can only help you learn, grow, improve, and get you to where you want to go.

Networking Exercise: Grow your network.

Grab a piece of paper, brainstorm, and write down the network of good people in your field that you already know. Then, do some research to find anyone interesting who may potentially be a good resource for you on your journey. Use the internet, talk to others and make yourself a list. Then, allot time during one day every week to work on growing your networking connections. This step includes anything from reaching out and introducing yourself to a new contact, wishing an existing contact a happy birthday, or just saying a hello and reconnecting with someone on social media or elsewhere. Start building and enhancing good networking relationships that will serve you on your path.

MISSION STATEMENT

Another highly productive way of keeping your definition of success veining through what you do is to create a mission statement. I had the opportunity to be actively involved with a high-level minor hockey team over the course of a few seasons, leading up to and through their Minor Midget draft year. During training camp, we worked together every day on defining success and figuring out how we would make it vein through our season. We spent time getting to know one another and fostering relationships. We set team goals and had discussions about what success looked like. We talked about the team's key ingredients, what they needed from one another and from their coaches, and what they thought their coaches needed from them. We discussed potential problems and conflict behaviours, and how we would handle them.

Through these conversations, we hit upon an interesting dynamic. It turned out there was one particular player who did not seem to buy into our process, and there was some conflict emerging as a result. As we worked together to deal with the conflict, something fascinating happened. The team started to become stronger and more united as a whole. The dynamic helped them to build their identity and recognize what they valued. At the end of the week, I helped the boys summarize the experience by creating a team mission statement. It was a culmination of all of the steps toward success we had worked on and were striving for, all neatly packaged into one statement. Here is the mission statement created by an insightful group of seventeen 15-year-old boys.

DON MILLS FLYERS 2000

We the 2000 Don Mills Flyers are a united front. We are a hardworking, committed, skilled, and physical hockey team that will strive for greatness. We will stay true to our teammates, our team goals, and our team identity. We build strength by coming together as one. We will put forth our best effort by going above and beyond the call of duty while holding ourselves and our teammates accountable. This is our game, our passion, our dream. It is in our blood. We will work hard, train hard, make good choices, and stay mentally tough. We will work through adversity effectively as we embark on our journey toward success. We are a brotherhood, and this is our time!!!

We had this inspiring mission statement printed on a sign and the boys hung it in their dressing room on game day, where they could see it each and every week throughout the season. They would take turns reading it before game time so they stayed connected to it. They knew their mission and would now never forget it.

As with any team, this one had its share of trials. They were up at times, down at times and plagued with injuries, but no matter what they faced, they remained a brotherhood. All of them but one. Remember that boy who was challenging us during training camp? He didn't last the season but the other boys were unified and strong. Still, there were bumps. When the team faltered, when people got down because they were losing or the season didn't seem to be going well, I worked to reconnect them to their mission statement. I would ask, "Are we doing these things? What have we lost sight of?" We would identify where the holes were and then we would work to fix them. When the boys managed to perform our identified tasks consistently, we found they would have great moments of success on the ice.

This team stayed together with a core group of kids over the years. At the end of their Minor Midget draft year, they made it to the semi-finals of the prominent OHL Cup tournament after winning two nail-biting double overtime elimination games along the way. These guys fought hard over the course of their journey together, as they battled through all of the adversity they faced. In the end, they didn't win it all, but they did fulfill their own definition of great success, along with experiencing the thrill of having eleven kids on the team drafted to the OHL that season. Some of these players are now moving on with full scholarship offers and commitments to Harvard, Boston University, Boston College, Providence, and Yale, as well as playing on different teams in the OHL and USHL, while pursuing their dream toward the NHL. Now that's greatness.

With these players currently in different cities and on different teams, sometimes even facing off against one another, the team remains one of the most special that I have ever encountered. It is also one of the most memorable they have ever been a part of. The bonds, the closeness, the caring and compassion they feel for one another, all remain strong. It is the definition of a true brotherhood, which veined throughout everything they did.

REDEFINING SUCCESS

As we go through life, things do change and so do people. We all develop—as a person, an athlete, a coach, a professional, a parent. Life happens and priorities shift. As a result, we sometimes need to redefine what success looks like and what it means for us. What success meant in the past might not look the same as it does today or what it will look like in the future. The fact that you may not be where you wanted to be right now doesn't mean you have failed to reach your goals. It means it's time to reevaluate your ever-evolving priorities so you can create a newly-fitting definition of success for yourself.

Years ago, my neighbour and close family friend, Lyle, came by for a visit. I knew he was a musician, but on this particular day, he actually sat down at my piano and started to play. I was blown away. He was just improvising, yet the energy, talent, music and vibe that he was exuding was mind-boggling. Over the years, we had many short conversations about his music career, and I had the opportunity to listen to music he had written and recorded with his band, but I had never heard him live. I could feel the rhythm running through his veins and coming out of every pore in his body.

Afterwards, we spoke in greater depth about his music career. I knew it was his passion. I knew he loved music, and I could see it. But, I could also see frustration and sadness in his eyes. He had spent years performing gigs and even playing for some famous musicians. He spent time writing and recording in his home studio. He even had some of his songs pass through the hands and ears of some very big artists like Aretha Franklin and Andrea Bocelli, but he had never gotten that one big career-changing break he wanted. He kept going, playing his music and following his dream. Life kept going as well. He got married and started a family, one baby after another, and then another.

With three small, beautiful children at home, he was faced with a dilemma. He had the opportunity to connect with some big names in the music industry and make a move to Nashville to advance his career, but he chose to stay in Toronto with his family. He has been married now for over twenty years and his kids have grown. Two of them have gone off to university and one is in high school, and they are all thriving. Lyle continues to work hard and is hands-down one of the best fathers I have ever met. Yet, his heart was heavy when he spoke about his music. It was his dream, and he felt like he didn't quite get there.

I asked him why he didn't make a move out of town to pursue his dream when he had the opportunity. That Nashville invitation was his chance to be in the right place, to be around the right people, and do the right networking to achieve his desired goal. He thought for a moment, and then explained that home was a better place for his family. While he could have gone to Nashville on his own, he knew his family needed him, and he did not want to miss watching his children grow up. He told me they were just too important to him to leave behind. So, he stayed home and played his music. He continued writing songs whenever he could find time between working, driving carpools, and running his kids to programs.

Together, we reflected on what he was verbalizing. Raising his family was this man's number one priority. All of his behaviours, sacrifices and actions were in line with that goal. He had made a choice. He did not fail in the music industry but rather, he succeeded as a husband and a father. To make it in the music industry, one has to do everything in line with what it takes to make it in music. To be a devoted husband and father, one has to do everything in line with what it takes to do that and that is exactly what he did. He achieved his success; it just needed a little redefining.

Today, Lyle continues to play his music and he continues to be phenomenal at it. And who knows. Maybe as life shifts once again, music will make it back to the top of the priority list and that big music opportunity is still to come. I would not be surprised.

> *"Define success on your own terms, achieve it by your own rules, and build a life you are proud to live."*
> **— Anne Sweeney, American Businesswoman, Past President of Disney Television, TV Director**

CHAPTER 8
WHY YOU DO WHAT YOU DO

THE WHOLE STORY

Here comes one of the most powerful questions I will ask in this book: **Why do you do what you do?** I am continuously pushing you to dig a little deeper, and we've been digging. But now I ask you, why do you get up every day and do what you do? Why are you reading this book? What drives you?

Now we are going right to the core. To the guts of who you are, what you are, what's important to you and why. This is where the passion lies. This is where you can accomplish anything. What drives me personally is greatness. I love being inspired by the greatness in others. I want to become the greatest version of myself, for me, for my children, for my family and for those I love. I love inspiring greatness in others and helping them become the greatest version of themselves. I love celebrating great moments of triumph and success, love, laughter and great connections. It gives me a rush and a thrill, and that's why I do what I do. That's why I am writing this book.

I didn't always have this knowledge about myself, and over the years, what drives me has changed. But helping others has been a consistent theme for me because it's in my nature. When it comes to determining your purpose, it can be helpful to start by looking at your nature and the general direction you follow as a result of it.

I grew up having a strong sense of care and compassion for people, perhaps because taking care of others has always been a consistent theme growing up. My two aunts were nurses and my mother stayed home and devoted her life to taking care of her family. Still today, my mom is all about family. That's what drives her. Throughout my childhood, my extended family—grandparents, aunts, uncles and cousins—were always around as well. Regular family dinners and get-togethers of 35 people were the norm for us.

In all aspects of life, though, you have to take the good with the bad. Growing up in a large, close-knit family was a great gift, but it also carried a burden. Everybody cared so much, and the support system was so large, that we were all in each other's business. As a teenager, I couldn't get away with anything because someone always found out and told someone, who told someone. Everyone knew everything and also thought they knew what was right for everyone else. We all felt each other's pain, so relationship boundaries were often blurred.

I consider it a gift to be blessed with a compassionate family and nature, but there have also been hard lessons I had to learn as a result. Out in the world, I have been lied to, pushed around, been taken advantage of, and gotten burnt out, because I tend to give too much and trust too much. But with each negative experience, I grew a little stronger and a little smarter. Once I learned to understand myself, I learned how to start using my passions in more productive ways. I learned to make them work for me and not against me. I realized that even as a youngster, I loved to help people. I worked with kids, I helped the elderly, and so it makes sense that I followed my passion into a field where I could help people. I give a lot. I get hurt a lot. But, I love what I do and I continuously learn. I constantly work to get better, to accept change, and to welcome growth. Doing what I love to do has driven my ultimate success.

*"The only way to do great work is to love
what you do. If you haven't found it yet,
keep looking. Don't settle."*
**– Steve Jobs, Co-founder, Chairman
and CEO, Apple Inc.**

THE BIG WHY?

I will ask the question once again: *Why do you get up every day
and do what you do?* Why do you play hockey, tennis, basketball, football, or baseball? Why do you work out in the gym, on the ice, or on
the playing field? Why do you sacrifice going out with friends and
eating junk food? Why do you spend hours of your time coaching
youth sports? Why did you choose the career path you are on? Why
did you start your business? Hopefully, when you strip away all of
the daily stress and the struggles, you can answer that you do the
work you do because you love it. Your answer should describe what
drives, excites, and inspires you. If it doesn't, why not? Your response
here may alert you that it's time to make some changes in your life—
within your sport, in your choice of work, or in your family. Maybe
it's time to change course and take a new path, or maybe, all you
need to do is change your approach to what you do.

We often get so roped into the hustle and bustle of daily life
that we forget about our *why*. We find ourselves simply going through
the motions, without stopping to reflect upon them. Of course, trying to answer the *why* question may feel like a daunting task. Maybe
you don't feel the passion, or you have forgotten the reason you started in the first place. Perhaps fear and stress have simply taken over,
or you've gotten caught up on life's treadmill. Perhaps you may have
been influenced by outside factors such as what other people think,
making it hard to figure out what you really love to do.

Regardless of why you are at an impasse, use this time to make a change. It could be taking time to reflect on some of the things you enjoy and consistently putting those things back into your sport, your workplace, or your life, like joking around with teammates, or making lunch plans with colleagues. It could be recounting the reasons you started doing what you do, or even creating new reasons to inspire you. It could mean it's time to begin a whole new journey pursuing your true passions and reinventing yourself. Whatever it is, start to do what you do with intent and bring some of that love and joy back into each day. You will be impressed by how much more fulfilled you will feel.

Reconnection Exercise: Reawaken the passion.

Here are some questions you can use to help you reconnect with what you enjoy about your sport, your work, or your life:

1. Why did you start your sport, your job, your business, or your family?

2. What do you or did you love about it?

3. What are the aspects of your life, your sport, your business, or your work, that you thrive in and enjoy?

4. What has interfered with the love and passion for what you do? What can you do about that?

5. What do you value? What do you love and feel passionate about? What makes you forget to eat or go to the bathroom? That's usually a good indicator that you are engrossed in and loving what you are doing. If you can't answer this question, then take a look back over the years and remember what you used to enjoy doing? Think about what you stand for. Think about where you feel

happy and alive.

If you haven't yet found your purpose, that's okay. Keep introspecting. This is an evolving process that starts with being mindful and acting with intention. A mentor of mine named Justin always says, *Do what you do with purpose, on purpose.* As for me, I always knew that I loved connecting with and helping people, but as I have said, my purpose has evolved along the way to get to where I am now. Here's how the process happened.

When I was a kid, I loved being with friends and family. I also loved to dance and play sports. My first love was hockey, but there was not much opportunity for girls to play hockey back then, so I played soccer instead. I enjoyed the game and being a part of my team. My team stayed together for a number of years, won the city championship, then a provincial championship, and eventually earned a spot to compete at the Canadian Nationals. Growing up, I also danced with a performance group composed of dancers, singers and musicians. Performing was a rush, but I especially loved the family-like atmosphere we developed from spending hours upon hours working together. Looking back, I am so grateful to have been a part of such a special group. I even returned for an alumni concert a couple of years ago. What a wonderful feeling to be back in the studio and back onstage with people I had developed such strong bonds with.

I didn't know it at the time, but as a kid, I was doing exactly what I loved to do: sports and dance, combined with a passion for being connected to people and collectively inspiring greatness around what we did. I was living my purpose, but that purpose was evolving. As a young adult, I studied psychology, then enrolled in a specialized honours dance program where I trained, performed, and learned about movement therapy. Then it was off to graduate school where I focused on counselling and psychotherapy. Upon graduation, I began working in a counselling practice helping people.

With time, knowledge, experience, and self-reflection, along with a willingness to get out of my comfort zone, my purpose evolved once again. I took my passion for sport and combined it with my work and aspirations to help people, and voila, my own specialized practice and company evolved. I finally did what I did with purpose and on purpose, and that intention has translated into the success of my practice. Staying true to my own passion and purpose is also what inspires success in those I work with. I feel proud and excited about what I have done. Of course, there are days that I am exhausted (actually, those are most days really), but when I am able to make a difference in someone else's life, I am re-energized by my purpose all over again. I can't stress enough the value of doing what you do with intention, finding your passion, and making sure that you know your why.

Target Thought: *Living with passion and purpose is a game changer.*

LIVE YOUR LEGACY

It has taken me many years and a lot of hard work to get to where I am today. I step back often and make sure to look at the big picture. My work has excited me, enlightened me, and given me the opportunity to make a positive impact. It has not come without stress, heartbreak, sadness, politics, a lot of bullshit, trash-talking, and craziness along the way. Thankfully, through it all, I have been fortunate enough to have seen, and continue to see, greatness along the way: moments of triumph, strength and determination, commitment and friendship, courage and passion, inspiration and success, and unforgettable examples of legacy.

There was a young hockey player named Alex who played

AA hockey for the Toronto Eagles. He seemed to eat, sleep and breathe the game. Alex was a happy kid, with lots of friends. He defined himself with these words: *I am a hockey player.* Alex's older brother played hockey on the same team as my son Brendan. These boys and their parents were a wonderful, compassionate family, and I felt lucky to call them dear friends. In the summer of 2011, Alex's mom was off to Australia for a business conference. Dad and the boys kissed her goodbye and were leaving the airport when Alex asked his dad if it was normal to have one leg larger than the other. Confused by the question, his dad took a look at Alex's legs, and fear set in. He knew something was wrong.

A slew of quickly arranged doctor appointments and medical tests ensued, and the news was not good. The diagnosis was undifferentiated sarcoma, a rare form of childhood cancer. All the while, Alex's mom was on a 20-hour flight to Australia. When she arrived, her phone rang, and she was on a flight back home. I remember her description of the moment she learned the news. It was a surreal experience. She could barely process anything her husband was telling her on that call.

There was no time to think. The doctors wanted to move fast. There were going to be major surgeries, rounds of chemotherapy and radiation ahead. The family was speechless. They didn't know what to say, ask, or do, as the doctors went on to describe the treatment plan. As Mom and Dad tried to find words, Alex had a question: "When I will I be able to get back to hockey?" Amidst all of the chaos, it was all he could think about. The doctor explained to his parents that the treatment would make Alex so weak, tired, and nauseous that he wouldn't be thinking about playing hockey for long.

The doctor was wrong. The questions about hockey never stopped. In fact, between bouts of surgeries, chemotherapy and radiation, Alex got into his hockey gear and began practicing with his team. He wore a green jersey to signal no body contact, as his blood levels were very low and any trauma could be a potential disaster for him. As chemotherapy can make bleeding potentially life threatening, Alex understandably didn't play during games. There was too much concern about his safety. His condition made body contact a significant risk factor. But despite all that was going on, there he was, back on the bench with his teammates, watching the game. Being there—in the place he felt he belonged— drove him. It helped him to get through his day-to-day battle with cancer. It gave him something to live for. In and out of hospital he went, yet he was determined to gain strength each and every time so he could get back to his team.

Then, one day, Alex was on his way to the hospital for another round of chemotherapy, but there were no beds available and he was turned away. That was great news for Alex. He went straight home, grabbed his hockey bag, swung it over his shoulder and off to the rink he went. He was so excited to get to the game on time. He asked his mom if he could get on the ice, even if it was just for the pre-game warm up. Alex's blood count happened to be good that day. Without telling anyone, his mom gave the coach the go-ahead to play him in the final shift, if the game was going okay. And there it was. As the clocked ticked down to the final minute of the game, Alex felt a pat on his shoulder. This young and courageous hockey player turned around to hear his coach say, "Grab your stick. You are going out there."

As Alex stepped onto the ice, the puck came his way on the boards and off he went. He cut in toward the net, wound up to shoot, and released the puck off the end of his stick. The crowd went silent, as though everyone was holding their breath as they watched the puck fly across the ice, sail past the goalie, and hit the back of the net. Alex had scored his first goal of the season. The eruption of cheering from the stands was thunderous. His teammates jumped up and down, screaming and rushing around him. You would have thought it was game seven of the Stanley Cup Finals. It was an unforgettable scene, not just for Alex and his family, but for every single person who witnessed it.

Alex's team made it to the conference finals that year, which is a pretty big deal. Unfortunately, though, it was time for another round of chemotherapy. Alex didn't want to go get treated. He wanted to be with his team for the final series. I remember his mother sitting with me in the stands one day. She didn't know what to do. Should she let him be with his team for the finals, or make him miss it to go to the hospital for chemo? I was shocked that she was even contemplating this possibility. I told her she needed to talk with Alex and tell him that he must get his treatment so that he could get better and play more hockey in the future. She got quiet. She looked at me with her beautiful, brown eyes, which were quickly filling up with tears, and she asked, "But, what if there isn't any more hockey for him in the future?"

I will never forget that moment. I felt like someone had punched me in the stomach. I guess I had been in denial and wanted to believe that everything would be okay. I never even considered the possibility that maybe it wouldn't. I didn't know how to respond. I hugged my friend, and we both cried.

At game 1 of the finals, Alex was at the rink. The decision had been made. It was an exciting and hard fought series with back and forth games between two great teams. It ended up in a do-or-die game 7 matchup and Alex was there with his team to play it. After battling with everything he had in him, he stayed and played with his team until that final whistle. Unfortunately, that game ended in a loss for his team, making it their last game of the season.

Nobody knew at the time, but over the course of the past weeks, Alex's cancer had been spreading with a vengeance. He never spoke a word about his pain until after that final game when he finally admitted to his parents that he wasn't feeling well. They took him to the hospital, and he never came out. He passed away two weeks later.

The memory of the masses of people who attended Alex's funeral will forever be etched in my mind. It was powerful to see all of his teammates there together, mourning for him. Then I watched as the entire opposing team from that final series walked in wearing their team jerseys to honour Alex, their young hero.

Alex was a very special young boy who had a purpose, and that was to play hockey. "It's like there is nothing else going on with me when I am playing hockey," he once said. When he could go to the rink, it allowed him to forget about the pain he was experiencing. Alex lived every second of his young life doing exactly what he loved to do. He lived his purpose. By doing so, he also inspired purpose in others. His team had a purpose, which was to play for him. He inspired purpose in all those who knew his story.

As a result of the dedication Alex showed on the ice, his story will be remembered in so many ways. His life created a legacy of determination, passion, respect, and ultimately, of grit. Known now as the Fighting Eagle, Alex inspired every player within the Eagles organization to wear a patch on their jersey with his hockey number on it. The patch is a symbol commemorating Alex and reminding each player within the organization to carry themselves with the same values and character by which he lived. As well, Alex is remembered at an annual hockey tournament called the Fighting Eagle for youth hockey players, which raises money for The Hospital for Sick Children in Toronto.

I share this story not to make you sad, but to inspire you to follow your passion and consider your own legacy. Throughout life's twists and turns, continue to forge ahead, create your legacy, and live it each and every day. Nothing changes until you do.

Legacy Exercise: Write your life story.

Take some time to think about how you want to be remembered. Imagine you are writing your own life story. What are some of the qualities you want to be remembered for? What beliefs or philosophies do you live by? What lessons have you learned that you want to share?

STAY CONNECTED

Once you have found your why, you have to make a deliberate effort to stay connected to it. You need to be in touch with the values that you bring to what you do and then live them in your day-to-day life. If you are an athlete, think about the love you have for your game. If you are a coach, remember when, why, and how it felt when you started helping people play the sport. If you are a corporate executive, consider the thrill of thriving under pressure, impacting people, and bringing skill together to collaborate toward a common goal. If you are a parent, remember your love and passion for raising a happy and responsible person. Whatever it may be, stay linked to your *why* every day. This feeling of connectedness is essential to good, healthy success, and it will serve as your lifesaver when the storms come, as they will. A great way to assist in developing this association is to create your own personal mission statement. Try it.

Mission Statement Exercise: Unite with your purpose.

Write a paragraph about who you are and what your mission is. Use the following points to help you organize your statement. You can also refer to the team mission statement above as an example and see how the points below were incorporated within it to help you get going.

1. State your current status and what you are striving for.
2. Create a statement about why reaching your goal is important to you.
3. Describe how you plan to achieve your goal.
4. List your own personal strengths and characteristics, the ones that you will draw upon to achieve your mission.
5. Make sure to use strong, positive and powerful language.

PRIORITIZE - PLAN - PREPARE

With your priorities and your mission set, wake up every morning and spend five minutes connecting to them. You want to start living each day with the behaviours and actions that support your mission. You can begin by looking at your agenda and removing all of the things that do not match your priorities. Work toward eliminating those daily activities, tasks, and people that get in the way of your objectives and replace them with things that connect you back to your purpose and mission. Next, plan your day with intentional actions that are in line with who you are and what you want. Now you are in the right position to set up whatever you need to in order make those things happen. Repeat these steps (prioritize - plan - prepare) until you finally eliminate everything that hinders you from moving toward your goals and living with purpose.

This process is not an easy one, but it will be worth the work. It's time to get out of "all talk" mode. You could have great plans, but if you fail to prepare for them, you fail to act upon them. You must have your prepared action plan in place to achieve the goals you set. It's easy to say you want to eat healthier, but if you have not gone shopping to buy the right foods, then it is impossible to change your diet. Know your priorities, plan your day and prepare for it. Then go out there and take charge of your day, one day at a time. When you do that, you take control and soon, the results you are looking for will become a by-product of your preparation and purposeful action. I speak the following tagline I learned from my mentor Justin both personally and to help my clients remember it:

Tagline: *Little by little, a little becomes a lot.*

Recently, I was fortunate enough to work with a AAA hockey organization that mandated all of their coaches to attend my training session. I had coaches from every team and every age group within the organization and I was excited to share my message with so many influential people. As the coaches began to arrive, I greeted them at the door and passed each one of them a cue card and a pen. I asked them to write down a few bullet points explaining to me why they do what they do. Before I began my talk, I collected all of the cards and away I went.

About halfway through my presentation, when I reached the part about knowing your why and staying connected to it, I pulled out those cue cards and began reading them out loud. The coaches wrote about positive experiences from the past and giving back to the game and sport. They wrote about being good role models and impacting the lives of young athletes. They wrote about development and helping players get better. They wrote about sportsmanship, developing character and teaching life lessons. They expressed their love for the game. Their answers were everything I wanted to hear. When I told them I thought it was amazing stuff, they smiled and nodded, quite proud of themselves. I told them they had all started coaching for the right reasons. Then, I asked a somewhat loaded question: "Do your day-to-day behaviours with your players and your team match those answers I just read off your cards?"

The room went silent. I paused before asking about those times when they yell at their kids. Do they know why they yell? Is there a teaching moment in there? How about the times when they sit those kids on the bench as a punishment because they made a mistake? Are they building character? What about when they play only their top guys because they need to win a game? Are they helping them to improve?

"Now, don't get me wrong," I told them. "I am just as competitive as the next guy. I like to win too. But interestingly enough, in response to the question, *Why do you do what you do?*, not a single coach in this room wrote *To win* on their cue card."

Believe me, I know there can be heated emotions in sport and in all high-stress environments, including the workplace and your personal relationships (of course, you can adapt the questions above to those areas of life as well). There is no doubt that sometimes tough decisions need to be made in high pressure situations and with respect to playing time at competitive levels, but are you making these decisions with purposeful action? For instance, when you bench a player, is there effective dialogue you have with them so the player understands what went wrong and can use the time to regroup and learn? When you yell at players, are you trying to build character in a purposeful way, or are you just letting your frustration and anger take over? When you are double and triple shifting your best kids without any regard for the other players on the team, are you promoting teamwork and sportsmanship? I went on to explain that while these are common instances in sport, they can be used in a better way as opportunities for learning—if they are connected to those valuable purposes on their cue cards.

The next day, one of the coaches called. He thanked me for my presentation and then shared that he had left feeling troubled. He was coaching for the right reasons, he explained, but he realized that the pressures of winning and his own frustrations were getting the best of him. He told me that he never really thought about the impact his yelling might have on the kids, but he didn't know how to change. He had no idea how to control his emotions when they came on. We talked some more about his personal reasons for coaching, including his priorities and how we could translate those into action. We prepared messages to offer the kids when they made a mistake, so that these moments could become teaching opportunities. We spoke about everyone on the team playing a role and encouraging growth, whether they were the best player on the team, or the worst player on the team. We discussed his own coaching preparation on game days and practice days.

Every time this coach went to the rink from that day forward, he set a plan for himself, choosing one small action that he wanted to accomplish that was in line with why he was there, and he followed it. Soon, he noticed positive results, not just for himself, but for the individual players and the team as a whole. All around, it has been a win-win situation and it stemmed entirely from intentionally bringing the right approach and seizing his opportunity to inspire greatness.

CHAPTER 9

REACH FOR THE STARS

THE DREAM COMES FIRST

We are all capable of achieving greatness in some form in our lives but to do so, we have to be able to believe in our dreams and then act on them. Too many people are afraid to dream big because of the belief that they can't get there, which stems from that underlying fear of failure.

My father helped me to believe in dreams. He showed me that he wasn't afraid to take a risk, even if things did not always turn out the way he had hoped. He believed in me and encouraged me to follow my dreams and not be afraid, even when I was not always on the right path. So, I am sharing his message. People often believe that the likelihood of their dreams coming true is slim, and the odds of what they want are not in their favour. Well, people do make it big in this life, so why not you? Stop selling yourself short. It's those who take the chance to reach for the stars, believe in them, and work for them that actually get there. If you can't dream enough to see your goal, then you definitely don't have a shot at achieving it.

Most people recognize the famous actor and comedian Jim Carrey. Well, Jim Carrey dreamt big. He did so before he was anybody you would ever know of. Did you know that Jim Carrey was broke and poor in the 1980s? He had nothing other than his dreams and aspirations. He used to find himself a frequent visitor in the self-help section of the bookstore, where he learned about the power of visualization. He would dream about becoming famous and he would visualize reaching his goals. One day when he was picturing the life he wanted, he did something I find fascinating. He wrote himself a cheque for $10,000,000 and dated it for Thanksgiving, 1995. Then he put that cheque in his wallet and kept it there for many years. It got crumpled and bent out of shape, but in his wallet it remained. He worked hard, audition after audition, and kept visualizing his success. The years rolled by, and then in late 1994, he landed the lead role in *Dumb and Dumber*—and just before Thanksgiving of 1995, he signed a ten-million-dollar deal.

One of the first questions I ask the people I work with is: *What are your goals? What do you hope to get out of what you do?* I tell them their answer can include anything. I learn very quickly who is all in, who is all talk, and who is hesitant and afraid to commit. I am always struck by those athletes who are in fact achieving success at their level of competition and are willing to do whatever it takes to get to where they want to be but are afraid to verbalize their dreams. They are hesitant to say that they want to compete in the Olympics, or win an Olympic medal, or play pro. So I push them a little further and a little harder, because they are doing the work, yet they seem to be holding back.

I ask them this question: *If I had a magic wand and I could wave it right now for you to achieve anything you want, what would it be?* I then start to see what people really dream of. Please, don't be afraid to reach for the stars and strive for excellence within your sport, your life or your career. You deserve success. If you do not dream big and don't strive for it, you will never get it. Period.

"The future belongs to those that believe in the beauty of their dreams."
– Eleanor Roosevelt, American Politician, Diplomat and Activist

BUILDING COMPETENCE

An essential requisite to effectively going after your dreams comes back to self-understanding and being able to recognize what you are and are not good at. Use your strengths to your advantage, and work your butt off to improve where you feel you are lacking. By this point, you have evaluated your skills and created your personal self-development plan. Use it. Work it, mould it, and slowly you will get better and develop a sense of competence. It's that simple. Building competence helps to foster belief and motivation, and a drive to continue. There will be setbacks along the way, but you have a new mindset to face them and grow from them, as you work to build the best version of yourself. If you sell yourself short, you've got no chance. GO FOR IT! If you fall or fail, you will learn. Remember that today is your day to get a little better. So away you go!

The strategy below is a quick and effective way to rebound from mistakes and setbacks. My athletes love this one and use it quite productively both on and off the ice or playing field.

Strategy: Find it, Fix it, Forget it

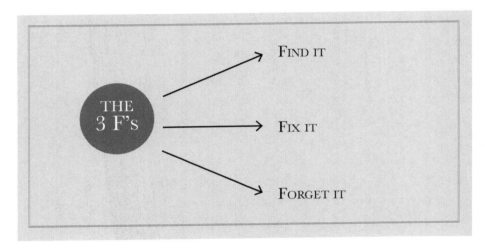

Step 1: F1- FIND IT
Figure out what it is that went wrong.

Step 2: F2 - FIX IT
Analyze what you can do to make it better for the next time.

Step 3: F3 - FORGET IT
With your new plan for fixing it set and ready to go, forget about the mistake and move on. I tell my clients they do not need to spend any more time on mistakes than that – especially when competing.

A female athlete named Anna reluctantly came to my office one day with her mother. I could see her apprehension. She did NOT want to be there. I told her I could understand her feelings; she was probably used to physical training, but not talking to someone about it. I joked around and let her know that I was totally used to athletes not wanting to talk to me, and she chuckled. I asked her why she came to see me, and she said her mother made her come. I smiled and said I was quite confident she would be the one asking to come back by the end of the appointment. She laughed. As it turned out, her mother had called me exactly one year earlier to book an appointment, but Anna had refused to come. Yet here she was.

I learned a lot about Anna during our time together. She was a high-level sprinter who had shown great promise and achieved great success for years, until she suffered a number of injuries. She was forced to take time off from training and competing and when she returned, some of her competitors had caught up to her race times and were beating them. This new reality was troubling. Then she suffered another injury. Coming back to the sport for the second time, the pressures and worries mounted, and Anna's performance started to deteriorate. Although she was still highly competitive, her times were slower than they had been and she viewed that fact as failure. Despite this setback, she had recently earned a full NCAA Division 1 scholarship to a very prominent Ivy League college in the U.S., which she is now attending. When I asked about her dreams, she told me that since she had achieved the scholarship offer, she didn't really have any other goals to work for. After pushing harder, I learned that competing in the Olympics used to be her goal, but it no longer felt like a viable option based on the way she was performing.

At the end of our session, I explained what I thought was happening and gave Anna my proposed game plan. In a nutshell, she viewed herself as a failure following her injuries because her times were off. She had lost her confidence, drive and motivation. She became increasingly fearful of failure and full of anxiety on race days. She dreaded competing and didn't want to be there anymore. She became more and more focused on her competitors, and more and more worried about letting down her coach and her mother. Anna was unhappy, unmotivated and full of doubt. She nodded, and it was clear that the insights I shared were bang on.

"Can you tell me how anyone could achieve success with all of those thoughts and behaviours going on?" I asked.

Anna nodded again and then she asked for the next appointment. We worked together to get Anna back on track (pun intended) and ready for college, with the goal of the Olympics right back at the top of her list. Perhaps even more important, she is engaged and excited for the first time in two years about getting better one day at a time.

Tagline: *I got this.*

STRIVE FOR EXCELLENCE

Every day, we all must strive to be better. No matter where you are, regardless of whether it is a good or bad day, or where your starting point is, just start and keep going. After someone wins a gold medal, the Super Bowl, the Stanley Cup, a Grammy, or the Nobel Prize, they don't quit. They still strive. The opposite is true as well. Whether you choked out there, failed a course, gave up that last big goal or point to give the opponents the win, blew that big deal at work, got bypassed for that promotion, or lost your cool at home, your job is to constantly strive to keep getting better.

Target Thought: *My job is to be better tomorrow than I am today.*

Strive for your own personal rendering of greatness. Reach for the stars. Stop judging yourself. Start evaluating your growth and progress on your quest toward continuous self-improvement. Here are three questions I teach all of my athletes and the others I work with to ask themselves in relation to their performance. They can be adapted to general day-to-day life as well:

1. What is one thing I did well at today?
2. What is one thing I can improve upon based on my performance today?
3. What is one thing I would like to focus on tomorrow or during my next performance?

Answering these questions on a regular basis helps to train the mind to find the positives in life, even when you don't feel them. You are also training your mind to find room for continuous growth even when things are going well. So ask yourself these questions at the end of every day, or after a game, competition, or performance. Like I said, it doesn't matter if it was a good day or a bad day, if you were brilliant or you sucked. You can always find (or create) something good to do, something you can improve upon, and something concrete you can focus on to move forward. If you don't get stuck in fear or judgment, you will always find a way to keep getting better.

"Success is not final, failure is not fatal, it's the courage to continue in both that counts."
– Winston Churchill, Prime Minister, United Kingdom

Develop your blueprint of excellence by continuing to build and work on yourself and your character. Do it with integrity and stay true to your core values as you make the push toward progress.

I equate this process with the life cycle of a tree. It all begins with a seed. The seed requires water and warmth in order for it to grow roots below the surface of the ground. The roots spread out and act as the anchor for the entire tree, providing its stability, and draw moisture from the ground so the tree can grow branches and leaves. Of course, the seed cannot grow unless it has the right ingredients, in the same way that you need your key ingredients in order to grow. The roots represent your own core values, your purpose and your why. They ground and stabilize you, and nourish the other aspects of your life. The trunk offers the tree its strength and delivers the moisture from the roots to the rest of the tree, symbolizing your personal strengths which support you in your life and in what you do. The main branches of the tree stand for the important appendages you must take care of, such as your health, your family and your relationships, while the extending branches represent your sport, your work, your school, your colleagues, friends and teammates. The leaves stand for all of the different experiences you have in your life.

Always remember, when the storms come, as they inevitably do, we rely primarily on what's under the ground to stabilize that tree—the roots. Branches can get damaged and break. Leaves change in colour, and they come and go. But with a solid core, you can rebuild and regrow what's on top. So, keep your core (values) strong. Whether the sun is shining, the winds are blowing, or the storm is strong, keep striving for excellence.

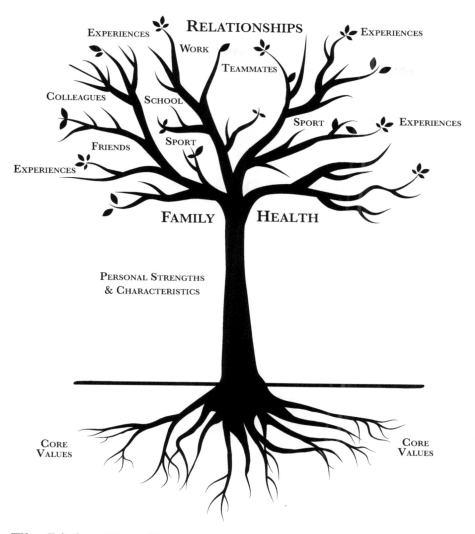

The Living Tree Exercise: Get rooted by creating your own living tree.

Note the corresponding aspects of your life, using your core values, traits, characteristics, work, sport, relationships and experiences, to create your own living tree.

SEE IT, BELIEVE IT, ACHIEVE IT

At this stage of the game, you have been working on creating a well-rounded picture to master your mind and generate your own blueprint for greatness. As I said earlier, this motto—*See it, Believe it, Achieve it*—is printed on the back of the T-shirts that my staff wear because it is a motto that I live by and I want veining throughout my company. I trust that by now you recognize that I believe anything is possible, especially if you can see it, believe it, and work your ass off for it. I believe you **CAN** achieve whatever you set your mind to with the right thinking and behaviours. To further boost your ability to get there, train your mind to use visualization techniques.

THE USE OF IMAGERY/VISUALIZATION

Visualization is an effective way to train the mind and build the mind-body connection. It is essentially a behavioural rehearsal, whereby you are laying the groundwork to help you attain your goal. If you can see and feel what you want, you will be better able to make it happen, just like Jim Carrey and so many others who have achieved great success. When you reach for those stars, having the power to see and feel them, as though you can touch them in the palm of your hand, can provide fuel for you as you pursue your goals and dreams.

Practicing visualization enables you to create that clear and detailed picture in your mind of what you want to play out in real life. This technique can also help you manage the stress that comes with attempting new, challenging things as it creates initial exposure and sets the stage for your desired performance.

Here are the overall benefits of exercising this technique as a regular part of your training and practice.

BENEFITS OF VISUALIZATION

- Improves focus
- Boosts confidence
- Enhances goal achievement
- Manages stress and pressure
- Helps gain control over emotions
- Reduces negative thinking
- Familiarizes self with scenario or competition
- Develops muscle memory
- Improves performance
- Perfects skills
- Reduces anxiety
- Conditions the brain

Visualization Exercise: See it, Feel it, Touch it.

- Close your eyes and breathe.
- Pay attention to your regular breathing pattern and get a sense of where your natural breath lives in your body. This will help you begin to focus inward.
- Begin to take deep, relaxing breaths, inhaling through your nose and exhaling through your mouth. With every exhale, clear your mind and blow away any thoughts, worries, or concerns of the day. Do so until your body starts to feel relaxed.
- Once relaxed, visualize your goals, what it is you want to accomplish and achieve. Create a description and picture of it. It can help to write yourself a script.
- Think about exactly how you want to be feeling, and try and create that feeling.
- Picture yourself doing what you are doing with confidence and ease.

- *Tip:* Use as many senses as possible when you create your script. Include touch, sight, sound, smell, taste. The clearer your picture, the more powerful the exercise becomes.
- Use strong, positive and encouraging language.
- Keep practicing and visualizing. The more you do it, the more adept you get.

Remember my friend Stan who ran the 100-mile marathon? As part of his mental game plan, he practiced imagery and visualization. Every night before bed, he followed an imagery script that took him through his run. He would imagine the adversity he would encounter and he would see himself pushing through with his plan in place and following the steps in his mind for dealing with leg cramps, nausea and vomiting. I even asked him to go to the organizers of the race and have them cut a small piece of the finish line for him to carry in his pocket. I knew there would be times during that race when he was breaking down and his mind would be so weak he would not be able to think clearly or rationally. I hoped that pulling out that finish line in those difficult moments would trigger his visualizations. I figured that if he could see himself crossing that finish line, he would be able to stay focused on his goal and mobilized to carry on. And it worked! So now it's your turn. See your finish line in your mind's eye so that you can move toward reaching it.

CHAPTER 10

CHOOSING YOUR HAPPY

BUILDING THE PLAN

From what I see, too many people have it backward. They are driven by the incorrect notion that success breeds happiness. They assume that when they become successful, when they get that athletic scholarship, sign a pro contract, or when they secure that big deal, build a multimillion dollar company, or get into their top choice university, that's when they will be happy. To that I scream: *NO! You've got it all wrong!* It's the other way around! Happiness breeds success.

We know that when you are happy and positive, you feel better. When you feel better, you act better. When you act better, you make better choices, bounce back from adversity faster, learn from mistakes and failure, believe more in yourself, give more, and actually enjoy the journey along the way. When you do all of that, success starts to breed itself. The good news is that happiness is a choice, if you decide to choose it. I understand that life will throw you curveballs. That's the way it goes. But what you can choose is your attitude toward it. Don't let life happen to you. Choose how you want to live it and how you want to respond to it. Take control of your own happiness.

"When one door closes, another opens; but often we look so long at the closed door that we do not see the one that has been opened for us."
— **Helen Keller, Author, Political Activist**

There is an extensive amount of research available that examines this happiness phenomenon. One summary study, by social psychologist Sonja Lyubomirsky and two of her colleagues, analyzed 225 different research studies on the topic of happiness and success. They found that people who reported being happy at age 18 achieved greater financial independence, higher occupational attainment and greater work autonomy by the age of 26. The study also showed that those who were happy as college freshmen had higher salaries 16 years later when they were 37 years old. So, the research supports that the happier you are, the more successful you will become, with a bonus of a higher potential income as well.

The benefits are clear. So are you ready to take control of your happiness? Let's discover how.

SHIFT YOUR PERSPECTIVE

When I was young child, my aunt told me a story that changed how I view happiness. When she was 18, she decided, against her family's wishes, to move to Vancouver. Her father kept harping on the downside: *What are you going to do there? It rains all of the time, how depressing. It's gloomy and grey. You will hate it!* In other words, what he was really saying was: Don't go! How's that for choosing happiness and focusing on the positives? Despite all of the not-so-positive feedback being thrown her way, she made up her mind. She wasn't going to let a few naysayers and a little or maybe a lot of rain, or anything else for that matter, stop her.

It was a busy time, but instead of packing, she headed out shopping. For what? What was so urgent that she needed to buy right away? When she came home, she unpacked her purchases. There it was! The brightest and happiest looking yellow raincoat and matching rain boots one could ever find. She now had what she really needed. It didn't matter how grey the skies were, or how much rain she had to endure; she would dress up in her bright yellow coat and boots and wear her own ray of sunshine wherever she went.

You need your own bright yellow raincoat and matching boots, too, and you need them today. Sport, life, climbing the corporate ladder, building a business, teaching, coaching, parenting…it's all hard. No matter what situation you may be faced with on any given day, you get to choose how you want to look at it. You must take control of where you place your focus. If you focus on the negatives, you will be miserable, reactive, and stuck in the victim role, letting things happen to you. Better yet, you can decide not to blame life, or circumstances, but rather do something about it and take back the power.

How do you do that exactly? If what is happening to you sucks, you now have a whole new toolkit of strategies, techniques, new thoughts, enhanced awareness and taglines to help you shift your perspective. Answer the W.I.N. question and choose a happy thought, a happy place, listen to some happy music, get the support you need, or help others in the same situation. Just change your focus and your perspective, and you will start to change your life.

For a number of years, I have been working with an American athlete named Lucas who plays hockey in the Western Hockey League (WHL). I have watched Lucas get drafted, get diagnosed with juvenile diabetes, get held back for a year as he learned to cope and adjust, and then finally play out his rookie year in the WHL. I have been lucky enough to watch him grow both as a person and as a player. After all he has been through, Lucas is doing great, but

FEARLESS - INSPIRING GREATNESS FROM WITHIN

there is one thing that consistently gets this kid down, and it is not the diabetes. It is his playing time on the ice.

After a fairly good hockey season last year, playing time was up and down throughout the playoffs, which started affecting his mood. His frustration over the situation began to impact his performance as well. I had Lucas ask the coach for feedback so he could figure out if there was something in particular he needed to improve upon, but he came up empty. Apparently, there was nothing missing from his game. The coach was just sending out his bigger, stronger, more experienced players. With nothing he could do to change the situation, Lucas found his frustration escalating with each practice and game. It got so bad that it started spilling over into his attitude, his body language and his play. His behaviour ended up earning him a talking-to from the coaching staff, and a healthy scratch for the next game. It doesn't help anyone to get stuck in the suck, and that's what Lucas was doing.

We needed a mental game plan, and fast. We discussed how to focus on working hard and practicing hard, and what that would look like. We created a plan for how Lucas could stay engaged during games when he was sitting on the bench. He would spend his time watching and learning from the guys getting ice time. He would also watch and analyze the players on the other team to learn where their strengths and weaknesses lay. This information would help his own personal development by enabling him to work and learn while sitting on the bench. It would also prepare him for when he did get out on the ice and would keep him from just sitting there, stuck in the suck.

For a while, this plan was working. Then Lucas' team made it through the playoffs and to the finals of the Memorial Cup. Everyone was excited, but not Lucas. Our whole plan, which had been working, was done, because all Lucas could think about was sitting on the bench while his teammates got to play in the Memorial Cup. I was having some trouble shaking him out of this mindset, despite the fact that he had all of the skills and knew what he needed to work on from a mental game perspective.

Lucas understood our mental game plan intellectually, but right now, he wasn't buying it emotionally. We had to find a way to break his negative cycle. I asked him to picture where he was at a couple of years ago when he was first diagnosed with diabetes. We talked about what it was like when he heard the news, and what it was like to learn how to eat and balance his sugars. I helped him remember what it felt like to get held back from going to the WHL and have to stay home and play another year of minor hockey with a team he didn't really want to be with. As we spoke, I could feel his frustration ease and his overall mood become more melancholy. Then I asked him, "If I had told you back then that you would have the opportunity to finish a good solid rookie season in the WHL and be a part of the team that went to the finals in the Memorial Cup, even though there wouldn't be much playing time in the playoffs, would you have jumped at the chance?"

He smiled and told me he would be have been all over that. And that is exactly where he was today. What Lucas deserved was congratulations. He had made it.

That was the turning point for Lucas. He shifted from being dejected to feeling happy and proud to be a part of the team and the experience. He went on to make the most of his time at the Memorial Cup and learned and grew as a result. He continues to learn and grow every day. His motivation level is currently very high, and he is working harder than ever. Without his frustrations holding him back, he is more committed to his goals within the game. His coach better watch out for him now! With a new perspective and some solid experience under his belt, Lucas is planning on arriving for year two as a bigger, stronger, and all-around better player.

Target Thought: *Circumstances are what they are, but I can choose my attitude toward them.*

THE HAPPINESS PLAN

Sometimes people lose sight of what makes them happy. In dark moments, everyone can get down about their situation and hyperfocus on the negatives. There are times for all of us when we can't seem to find that better place to put our focus or figure out how to shift our perspective. That's why it's so important to take the time to equip yourself for that eventuality beforehand. If you do some work now, you will be armed and ready to deal with difficult moments when they happen.

Consciously do some of the things that bring happiness and joy into your life. Turn on your favourite music. Watch a movie that interests you. Find someone inspirational and listen to their story. Read a great book. Talk to someone who makes you feel wonderful about who you are. Be kind to others; be kind to yourself. Think of someone you admire. Think of a place you love or an activity you are passionate about. Get connected to whatever makes you feel good. Create a whole bank of these happy things. Keep building that bank and making deposits into it. Know all of the good things, memories and people in your life, and draw upon them whenever you need.

If you are facing some adversity in your life right now, then take some time to develop your happiness plan to help deal with it. At times, pain can run so deep that you don't know what to do or how to move through it. You may have to endure it, feel it, and grieve. No matter how bad things get and how lost you may be, having a plan to rely on and focusing on that plan can help to provide a source of strength during troubled times.

The Boston Marathon was a day of hope, inspiration, work ethic and great spirit. In April of 2013, people set out to destroy that. It turned into a day of horror and chaos as two bombs went off at the finish line, the place where innocent runners were steps away from accomplishing their goals, and hundreds of spectators stood along the sidelines, cheering them on. Sadly, there are countless moments of pain and suffering like this one throughout history, but there is inspiration for us in there somewhere, as in the story of Jessica Kensky and Patrick Downes.

This vibrant, newly-married couple was enjoying a day off, standing at the Boston Marathon finish line, when the bombs went off. Jessica, who lost both of her legs, and Patrick, who lost one of his, both describe that day as being the worst thing and the best thing that has ever happened to them. Imagine finding that perspective after such a tragedy. How did they do it?

Kensky and Downes chose not to focus on their pain and all they have lost, but rather on what they have gained: the bonds, love and support they have received since. That perspective gives them the strength to survive and continue living. They have even devised a plan to work toward celebrating and demystifying the journey of the disabled. Hard at work defining new successes and happiness every day, they wrote a children's book called *Rescue & Jessica*, which chronicles the love story between Jessica and her service dog.

Through their experience, these trauma survivors have become both mentally and physically stronger, and three years after the bombing that disabled them, they returned to the Boston Marathon finish line to celebrate their triumph. Despite having lost his leg and learning to not only walk again but also run again, now with a prosthetic leg, Patrick crossed the finish line as a runner this time, not a spectator. His wife, Jessica, was there for an emotional embrace as he finished.

There is no doubt that after that fateful race, life as this couple once knew it would never be the same, and their new reality was tragic and frightening. At the same time, their strength and courage since that day is something we can all learn from. Patrick and Jessica continue to celebrate what they have and what they gained, rather than what they lost. They have proven to themselves and the world that adversity cannot break their spirit. That is their choice, and they probably have to work to choose it every day in order to make it happen. That is how they survive their trauma and move on to build their own happiness and success.

Learn from their story, and try the additional techniques below to further evolve your own personal happiness plan.

GET SUPPORT

We already know the importance of surrounding yourself with positive and supportive people as a motivating force in your pursuit for personal greatness. These people are also vital to your happiness plan because they generate overall positivity. Having a strong support system means you have people in your network who are there to back you as you work toward your goals and who can help you pull through in times of trouble. Don't be afraid to reach out to your trainers, mentors, teachers, doctors, therapists or any other supportive people you can count on. It is important to both recognize and access the right sources of support when you need it. Asking for help is a sign of strength and courage, not weakness.

I am so fortunate to have the undying support of my family and extended family, along with special friends who are always there to back me in whatever I do. I have to thank each and every one of them for being in my corner as I work toward my success. I also had the advantage of having parents who cheer me on throughout my life, helping me to believe in myself. Make sure to find and surround yourself with those people who make you feel like there is nothing you can't accomplish.

MAKE YOUR BED

This next technique, which I learned from Navy Seal William McRaven, works to help set the right tone to move forward and reach your goals every day. It may sound silly but it's actually very effective. Make your bed in the morning. When you get up and make your bed, it is a sign that you are getting everything in order and ready to start the day off right. You are kicking off your day and taking control to establish a good routine.

Making your bed is a little thing, but doing it with purpose can lead to feeling accomplished, which is great ammunition to help you take on the bigger tasks ahead. As you pull and smooth and tuck, be intentional, knowing that you are getting everything straightened up and into place. Equate clean corners with a clean start. As you tuck that last corner in, feel good about it and remind yourself that you are ready to go and attack the day.

Even when things may be falling apart around you, make your bed! And at the end of day, enjoy getting into that freshly made bed that feels so much better than a messed up one.

SMILE

The next little thing I want you to deliberately make an effort to do is smile. A little smile can go a long way. Have you ever heard that yawning is contagious? It has been said that if you yawn, someone else is likely to yawn too. I think smiling is contagious as well, so I tried it. I walked around the streets and started smiling at random people. If they didn't think I was out of my mind (it's all a matter of perspective of course), they would usually smile back. As it turns out, I'm not so far off after all. There is research out there confirming that not only is smiling contagious, but it also makes you appear more attractive.

Further research shows us that smiling impacts the activity in our brain. It activates the release of tiny molecules that fight off stress. It also releases our feel-good neurotransmitters, such as serotonin and dopamine, which help to relax stress, make you feel good, and even reduce pain. And when you smile at someone else, you create a symbiotic relationship, whereby their brain coaxes them to return the favour. Now both people activate those reward centres in the brain and set off the same feel-good chemicals. So, try it sometime and help yourself feel good.

Just as smiling is contagious, so is complaining. In fact, research has shown that, unfortunately, our brain reacts more strongly and holds on to negative stimuli far more tightly than it does to positive ones. That may be why we tend to find so many people focusing on the negatives. It is believed that a negative experience gets stored instantly in the brain, while a positive one must be held in the mind for 12 seconds before it is stored. Well, that's not the best news. Are we hardwired to be complainers? To that I ask, *who cares?!* Let's just work with it, because we also know that the brain is considered to be "plastic". Based on the science of neuroplasticity, we know that the brain has the ability to change itself. Really, all we have to do is focus a little longer on the positives and smile a little more often to activate the happy parts of our brain, and we will be good to go. We will have stored positivity into our memory. So, spend more time smiling. Put more effort into speaking positives to yourself and to others, and they will likely return the favour. The more positivity you can bring into your life, the more it gets etched into your mind.

CELEBRATE SUCCESSES

We all spend way too much time ruminating on what's going

wrong and not nearly enough thinking about what is going right. A great strategy to boost your happiness quotient is to make a persistent effort to celebrate both yours and others' successes—and not just the big milestones but the little successes as well. Like the time when you finally got some power into that slapshot of yours, or that one shift you did get out there for the power play, or that first win amongst a heap of losses. As a parent, you want to stop and celebrate your child's *I love you* amidst sleepless nights and the busyness of raising a family. Stop and give yourself a pat on the back when you get a good grade or sign a contract or write a book. Remind yourself how hard you have been working at it, and give yourself some kudos for a job well done.

Instead of allowing our failures to embody us, while we allow ourselves only brief moments of happiness, we have to train ourselves to milk those celebratory moments and keep building upon them. Doing so will mean spending more time being happy and feeling good while shifting perspective in a positive direction. Celebrate birthdays, milestones, big successes and small successes. They are all noteworthy, so don't let them slip by unnoticed.

Let me circle back to that special hockey team I worked with, the one that formulated its own mission statement to live by. Together, we worked hard to create a culture of excellence and a family-like atmosphere that was uniquely special. Through our process, we decided that we wanted to find a way to celebrate successes throughout the season. The kids did some brainstorming and came up with an interesting plan that would make every teammate feel special.

Every month, we would do something to celebrate each player who had a birthday during that month. It wasn't a huge deal. We would bring a little treat and some birthday candles into the dressing room after a game or a practice. I definitely took a little slack from the coaching staff because it was often cupcakes or donuts...too much sugar! But, we did it anyway. Although the boys always looked forward to a treat, what made the exercise special was going around the room and hearing each player say something about their teammates who were being celebrated that day. The guys would share an attribute that they liked or admired about them as a person, or as a hockey player.

I was fortunate enough to be a part of this activity at the beginning, and I remember being touched by some of the words spoken. They were a somewhat rowdy group of teenage boys who had strong minds of their own and some attitude to go along with it. But their words to their teammates were kind and thoughtful, with some jokes and fun mixed in as well. Everyone had a chance to be on the giving as well as the receiving end of the celebration, creating a profound and lasting impact on all who took part.

BE GRATEFUL

Practicing gratitude is one of my favourite exercises. The act of giving thanks can help to rewire your brain and generate happiness. I should know. About five years ago, I started on this "being grateful" kick. I would preach gratitude here and there with some of my athletes who I felt needed it, and I started getting some good results and feedback. It seemed to be helping people feel good and work hard. Soon, I started wondering why I wasn't practicing gratitude on a regular basis with all of my athletes, with my family, and in my own life.

It was a cold winter day in Canada, one of those days that starts when you wake up in the dark and ends when you come home in the dark. The sun rose at 7:40 a.m. and set at 4:40 p.m., even though there was no sunshine on that particular day. I was in the office all day, but had a two-hour meeting that got cancelled. There was still a lot of work to catch up on, but the gloomy weather was getting to me so I decided to start practicing gratitude. I took a moment, just a moment, to recognize how grateful I felt that I had this newly found two-hour break in my day, which gave me some free time, an opportunity to do what I wanted to do. I picked up my purse, ran outside, jumped into my car and drove to pick up my kids from school. Usually, my kids took the school bus home, but I thought, *Wow, I have this break. It would be nice to see them and so fun to surprise them.* So, off I went. I played some of my favourite music in the car, sang along, and before I knew it, I was smiling outside their school. What a shift!

When my kids got into the car, they didn't look so happy. They were kind of in the same place I had been earlier, dark and gloomy, like the weather. They were quiet, grunting out responses to my cheery "How was your day?" But I was not going to let them bring the dark clouds into the car, so I decided to try the whole gratefulness thing on them. I told them what I had been working on, and explained that together, we were going to start practicing being grateful. They grunted some more and seemed annoyed, but I pushed them. I told them they each had to tell me something they felt grateful for today.

"Nothing," they both answered, then proceeded to complain. "I have two essays due this week and a big test tomorrow. I had a long, boring day at school and now I have to go home and study all night," Brendan blurted out, while Noah just sat there, silent.

"Sounds like it has been and will continue to be a long day," I said. "I would still however, like everyone in this car to tell me what they are grateful for."

Both kids sat there, moping. So, I told them they had the ride home to come up with something, but no one was getting out of the car until they answered the question. As the car turned the corner of our street and approached our house, I drove right by it. All of a sudden, the boys yelled out, "What are you doing?!"

I calmly repeated, "I told you we are not getting out of the car until you answer my question."

They realized I meant business. There were a few more grumbles, along with a lot of eye rolling while I remained calm and kept driving. Finally, Brendan broke the silence. His voice softened as he said, "Well, I guess I am grateful that you picked me up from school today. It was a hard day and I still have a lot of work to do, but you just gave me an extra 40 minutes because I didn't have to ride the school bus. I guess I can use that extra time at home to have a snack and a little break to recharge before I get back to my work, so thank you for that."

I thought, *Wow, that was amazing,* and I felt even happier. I could also feel that the mood of the car was shifting. Next, Noah spoke up. "I forgot that I got a good mark on a big presentation that I worked really hard on and I did very well, so I guess I am grateful about that."

And there it was. Practicing gratitude is a gift you can give yourself. By pushing to find something to be grateful for, we all shifted our perspective and felt happier. I went back to work smiling and had a rewarding session with one of the teams I worked with. Brendan took a break and then got right down to work while Noah felt proud of himself and told me he couldn't wait to get started on his next presentation. And it all happened on this dark, cold, winter day.

Gratitude Exercise: Give thanks for what you have.

Once a day, every day, fill in the blank.

Answer and speak the following statement: Today I am grateful for

_____

_____

DO WHAT YOU LOVE

The greatest way to build happiness in your life is to engage in the things that actually make you happy. Do what you love and you are passionate about, and connect to it on a regular basis. Follow your dreams. The more you engage in the things that drive happiness, the more you will foster success in whatever it is you are doing. Find ways to incorporate more of what you love into your life, your teams, your school and your work. Enjoy great food, great books, great movies, fun activities, great people and great conversations. Show love for the people you care about, and allow yourself to be loved in return. Whatever it is, find it and do it. Don't wait.

PRACTICE TRUST AND HUMILITY

As you build your plan for personal greatness, you must trust in yourself that you can go out there and execute it, step by step. Be confident and strong, remembering that greatness is possible, no matter where you are kicking things off from. Work to become the greatest you that you can be. Trust in the process. And as you do so, always remain *humble*. Life is a privilege, and your time here on earth is fleeting. It is up to you to live each day in the best way you know how. Face your fears and go out there with your new fearless approach.

I once had the great honour of listening to, learning from, and speaking with Sir Graham Henry, who is considered to be one of the most outstanding coaches of all time. He was successful in transforming the All Blacks, New Zealand's National Rugby Team, into a culture of excellence. Today, the All Blacks are revered as the most successful sports team in the world throughout history.

Coach Henry spoke about so much that day. He spoke about his purpose, which was to create the best sporting team in the world.

He spoke about the principles that he used to build that success by fostering a positive culture within his team. He spoke about figuring out the keys to success and then implementing them. He spoke about greatness being built with people and connection, and responsibility and accountability, and constant self-improvement. His words were impactful and inspirational. But the one thing that stood out to me most was his sense of humanness and humility. There he stood, having achieved unbelievable levels of success within himself and his team, and yet he quickly pointed out his mistakes and shortcomings. "I wasn't the best. I just worked my ass off," he said.

Coach Henry's path to success began with self-awareness. He told a funny story about his pre-game speeches. He recalled how he would set out to inspire his players and then strut out of the locker room feeling so pumped up and proud. He thought he had the gift of delivering the most uplifting and stimulating speeches ever, until one day, when one of the guys had the courage to tell him that his speeches were "sh*t". In fact, everyone on the team hated them. He laughs about it now, but at the time, this revelation forced him to figure out what the problem was. After some reflection, he realized that the words in his speeches were not connected to the players and where they were at all. They were for himself. That realization taught him so much. "I wasn't self-aware until I was 58 years old, but I am now," he told us.

The Coach's message was clear. You can always learn at any point in your life; it is never too late to grow. Just stay humble so you can self-reflect and figure out what works best.

FINDING YOUR FEARLESS

Throughout the pages in this book, I have asked you to focus inward and learn about yourself, so you can begin carving your own personal path to greatness, without fear holding you back. To get there, I have asked you to pay attention to many things. I have asked you to gain awareness, understand your own mindset and work to change unproductive thinking. I want you to manage your expectations and replace them with a focus on the process. I want you to work hard. I want you to build your confidence and your belief in yourself even in the face of fear. I want you to define your own success. I want you to know the *why* behind what you do. I want you to reach for the stars and know what to do when you fall short. As you work to create your own happiness and success, I want you to trust that you will find it. This work may or may not feel overwhelming, depending on where you are at in your life right now, but you can do it.

Choose one thing in this book to focus on, like making your bed in the morning, or creating a vision board, or drafting a mission statement. Pick one purposeful task and get going. The truth is, there are so many great motivational speakers and self-help books out there all waiting to inspire you. At the end of the day however, the greatness lies within you. I may have all of the right things to say and teach, but they are just words until you put them into action. When you are willing to do that, day in and day out, that's when you will begin creating something special.

It is not about reading this book; it is about embracing the concepts within it. It is about searching for your purpose, and living each day honouring that. It is about continuous growth and learning, facing fear, shifting your mindset and taking action toward your goals, one day at a time, every day, for the rest of your life. If my buddy Stan could cross that finish line after 100 miles, so can you.

Remember, do what you do with purpose and with everything you've got. Whether you are an athlete, a coach, a parent, a teacher, a business executive, a student, or anything else, give your best effort and trust in your own greatness. It is inside of you to nurture.

And one closing message for you…

Always remember to play to the final whistle.

Know it. Believe it. Prepare it.
Face the fear. Work for it.
Fall down. Get up.
Regroup. Prepare again. Rebuild.
Refocus. Get better. Try again.
Be purposeful. Stay connected. Be humble.
Take another hit. Get back up.
Repeat until you Succeed.

REFERENCES

Andal, Elizabeth. "10 Famous Failures That Will Inspire You to Be a Success." Lifehack.org, n.d. Web. http://www.lifehack.org/articles/communication/10-famous-failures-that-will-inspire-you-success.html

Associated Press. "Brady, Patriots stomp Steelers, reach 7th Super Bowl under Belichick." FoxNews.com, 22 January 2017. Web. http://www.foxnews.com/sports/2017/01/22/brady-patriots-stomp-steelers-reach-7th-super-bowl-under-belichick.html

Brian, Denis. "Einstein: A Life. Chapter One: Childhood and Youth." *The Washington Post,* 1996. Web. http://www.washingtonpost.com/wpsrv/style/longterm/books/chap1/einstein.htm

brom3780. "Best Sports Teams of All Time." TheTopTens.com, n.d. Web. https://www.thetoptens.com/best-sports-teams/

Brophy, Mike and Todd Denault. *Unbreakable: 50 Goals in 39 Games: Wayne Gretzky and the Story of Hockey's Greatest Record.* McClelland and Stewart, 2016. Print.

Ciotti, Gregory. "5 Scientific Ways to Build Habits That Stick." *99u. com,* n.d. Web. http://99u.com/articles/17123/5-scientific-ways-to-build-habits-that-stick

Duckworth, Angela et al. "Personality Processes and Individual Differences, Perseverance and Passion for Long Term Goals", *Journal of Personality and Social Psychology, 2007,* Vol. 92, No. 6, 1087-1101 https://www.sas.upenn.edu/~duckwort/images/Grit%20JPSP.pdf

Fox, Kit. "Patrick Downes Becomes First Boston Bombing Amputee to Finish Marathon." *RunnersWorld.com*. 18 April, 2016. https://www.runnersworld.com/boston-marathon/patrick-downes-becomes-first-boston-bombing-amputee-to-finish-marathon

"Gaylord Perry." *Wikipedia, The Free Encyclopedia*. 17 September 2017. Web. https://en.wikipedia.org/wiki/Gaylord_Perry

Gretzky, Wayne and Rick Reilly. *Gretzky: An Autobiography*. Harper Collins, 1991. Print.

Guerra, Cristela. "The Story of Rescue and Jessica, A Dog, A Woman, & Rebirth". *BostonGlobe.com*, 27 October 2016. https://www.bostonglobe.com/metro/2016/10/26/the-story-rescue-and-jessica-dog-woman-and-rebirth/2BNCPzxcvJKOmvvLVol9MJ/story.html

"J.K. Rowling Biography.com". *Biography.com*, A&E Television Network, 27 April 2017. Web. http://www.biography.com/people/jk-rowling-40998#fame-and-fortune

"Johnny Manziel." *Wikipedia, The Free Encyclopedia*. 24 September 2017. Web. https://en.wikipedia.org/wiki/Johnny_Manziel

Knox, Kristopher. "Super Bowl 2017 Score: Quarter-by-Quarter Breakdown of Patriots vs. Falcons." *BleacherReport.com*, 5 February 2017. Web. http://bleacherreport.com/articles/2691348-super-bowl-2017-score-quarter-by-quarter-breakdown-of-patriots-vs-falcons

Lane, R.D, and Lynn Nadel (Eds.), "Neural correlates of levels of emotional awareness. Evidence of an interaction between emotion and attention in the anterior cingulate cortex", *Cognitive Neuroscience of Emotion*. New York: Oxford University Press, 2000. 345–370. Print.

Lyubomirsky, Sonja. "Happiness Breeds Success...and Money!". *Psychology Today.com*, 18 July 2008. https://www.psychology-today.com/blog/how-happiness/200807/happiness-breeds-success-and-money

O'Doherty, J. et al. "Beauty in a smile: the role of medial orbitofrontal cortex in facial attractiveness", *Neuropsychologia*, 2003, Vol. 41, Issue 2, 147-155. Print.

Parsell, Ken. *The Catalyst of Confidence: A Simple and Practical Guide to Understanding Human Potential.* Parsell Enterprise Group, 2011. Print.

Romano, Andrew. "The Beatles Succeeded Through Talent, Ambition, and a Lot of Arrogance." *TheDailyBeast.com*, 10 November 2013. Web. http://www.thedailybeast.com/the-beatles-succeeded-through-talent-ambition-and-a-lot-of-arrogance

Stevenson, Sarah. "There's Magic in Your Smile: How Smiling Affects Your Brain", *Psychology Today.com*, 25 June 2012. Web. https://www.psychologytoday.com/blog/cutting-edge-leadership/201206/there-s-magic-in-your-smile

Thompson, Phil. "Fan gets Super Bowl date with Genie Bouchard, hopes for second." *Chicago Tribune.com*, 16 February 2017. Web. http://www.chicagotribune.com/sports/chicagoinc/ct-genie-bouchard-super-bowl-bet-date-20170216-story.html

"Tom Brady." *Wikipedia, The Free Encyclopedia.* Wikipedia, The Free Encyclopedia. 25 September 2017. Web. https://en.wikipedia.org/wiki/Tom_Brady

"What Oprah Learned from Jim Carrey." *Oprah.com,* 12 October 2011. Web. http://www.oprah.com/oprahs-lifeclass/what-oprah-learned-from-jim-carrey-video

Williams, Ray. "Are We Hardwired to Be Positive or Negative?", *Psychology Today,* 30 June 2014. Web. https://www.psychologytoday.com/blog/wired-success/201406/are-we-hardwired-be-positive-or-negative

Made in United States
Orlando, FL
22 August 2022